Pelican Books
Soviet Education

Nigel Grant was born in Glasgow in 1932, and was
educated at Inverness Royal Academy and Glasgow
University, where he took an M.A. in English in 1954.
He then trained as a teacher and, after two years in
the army, taught in Glasgow secondary schools,
studying for the M.Ed. at the same time. In 1960
he joined the staff of Jordanhill College of Education
in Glasgow, and in 1965 was appointed Lecturer in
Education at the University of Edinburgh. During his
thirteen years there, he developed courses in
comparative education, completed his Ph.D., became
Reader in 1972 and latterly head of the Department
of Educational Studies. He returned to the
University of Glasgow in 1978 on appointment to the
Chair of Education. Other commitments have
included the chairmanship of the British Section of
the Comparative Education Society in Europe and of
the Scottish Educational Research Association, and
four years as editor of the journal *Comparative
Education*. He has also travelled extensively,
lecturing in the U.S.A., Canada, Denmark, Germany,
Ireland and Egypt, and has conducted field studies
in these countries and elsewhere in Western Europe,
in the U.S.S.R., and in all the countries of Eastern
Europe except Albania. His other writings include
various papers on comparative education, a book on
the school systems of Eastern Europe and, with
R. E. Bell, *A Mythology of British Education* and
Patterns of Education in the British Isles. Other
interests include poetry, politics, music, natural
history and linguistics. Professor Grant is married
with two children.

£1·80

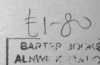

BARTER BOOKS
ALNWICK STATION
NORTHUMBERLAND

Nigel Grant

Soviet Education

Fourth Edition

Penguin Books

Penguin Books Ltd, Harmondsworth,
Middlesex, England
Penguin Books, 625 Madison Avenue,
New York, New York 10022, U.S.A.
Penguin Books Australia Ltd, Ringwood,
Victoria, Australia
Penguin Books Canada Ltd, 2801 John Street,
Markham, Ontario, Canada L3R 1B4
Penguin Books (N.Z.) Ltd,
182–190 Wairau Road, Auckland 10, New Zealand

First published 1964
Second edition 1968
Reprinted 1970
Third edition 1972
Fourth edition 1979

Copyright © Nigel Grant, 1964, 1968, 1972, 1979
All rights reserved

Made and printed in Great Britain by
Richard Clay (The Chaucer Press) Ltd, Bungay, Suffolk
Set in Monotype Plantin

Except in the United States of America, this book is
sold subject to the condition that it shall not, by way
of trade or otherwise, be lent, re-sold, hired out, or
otherwise circulated without the publisher's prior
consent in any form of binding or cover other than that
in which it is published and without a similar condition
including this condition being imposed on the
subsequent purchaser

Contents

Contents

Contents

Preface

This book seeks to present a bird's-eye view of Soviet education today. For the most part, I have tried to concentrate on the facts and keep conclusions to a minimum; but since it is almost impossible to write on any aspect of life in the U.S.S.R. without touching on the controversial, and since facts can be called in question no less than conclusions, it would be as well to declare my sources at this stage. As well as making use of the accounts of other visitors to the Soviet Union, I have drawn on my own impressions of schools, colleges, and other institutions in Moscow and Leningrad in September 1962, Moscow and Minsk in April 1968, and Moscow, Kiev, and Erevan in February 1976. On these occasions I watched lessons and attended lectures, visited many kinds of educational establishment, and had many discussions with teachers, lecturers, professors, students, youth workers, parents, and officials at ministerial and local level. Most of these meetings were officially arranged, but others which arose from chance encounters were both informal and informative.

But this, useful though it has been, would not be enough; there are limits to what the visitor can learn, however fortunate in his contacts. Visits can put flesh on the bones of hard information, and most of this has to be obtained by other means. Fortunately, there is a wide range of Soviet material available in the West – official documents and statistical accounts, books, specialist journals, and articles in the general Press; all these can yield a great deal of information, not only about what the system is supposed to do, but about many of the problems and shortcomings as well. I have also used the writings of British, German, and American observers, many of which are painstakingly thorough and highly perceptive. Taking Soviet and Western sources together, there is enough material on education in the U.S.S.R. to fill several books the size of this.

Preface

The information is nevertheless incomplete, and sooner or later the investigator is faced with some uncomfortable gaps in his knowledge. There is usually no problem in finding out what is supposed to happen in the schools; and it is usually easy enough to find *some* cases where the practice does not measure up to the theory. But it can be extremely difficult to discover just how widespread the shortcomings are, and collecting complaints can give just as misleading an impression as accepting everything in the official accounts at face value. Every statement has to be checked against something else, and still there are gaps in the picture. I have tried to remedy this as far as possible by piecing together clues from various sources, by picking the brains of friends and colleagues, and sometimes by falling back on my own impressions. Ironically, in some ways there is too much original material; to monitor the Soviet educational Press alone would be a full-time job for a fast reader, and selection – which necessarily means an element of chance – is absolutely necessary. For these reasons I have tried to stick to the facts; and where these are in dispute, I have tried to make this clear in the text. I have also dropped in the present edition some material that was used in previous ones concerning precise costs; it is still available, but such is the pace of change in monetary values that information of this kind is likely to date too fast for it to be of much help.

My task has been made much easier by many people who, directly or indirectly, consciously or unconsciously, have supplied material that has found its way into this book, both in its original and subsequent versions. I should like to express my indebtedness to the Academy of Pedagogical Sciences of the U.S.S.R., to the Ministries of Education of the R.S.F.S.R. and the Byelorussian S.S.R., to the Institute of Pedagogy of the Ukrainian S.S.R., and to other Soviet bodies for information and documentation not readily available elsewhere, and to the many teachers, pupils, students, lecturers, and officials whom I watched in action and who showed themselves extremely helpful in the face of often lengthy questioning; to the Hayter Foundation and the Scottish Council for Research in Education, for financial support of some of the field research; to the East European Section of the U.S. Office of Education, Washington D.C., for the loan of documents; to Professor G. H. Read, of Kent State University, Ohio, for information and access to files; to Professor W. M. Cave, of the University of Michigan, for information on the education of national minorities; to many German colleagues, in particular Professor Dr O. Anweiler, Professor Dr W. Mitter, and Professor Dr D. Glowka, for information and ideas on many occasions; to my colleagues in Eastern Europe for a wealth of information, written and oral, over the past few years; and to colleagues and friends in the United Kingdom who have provided information, facilitated contacts, made suggestions, and sparked off ideas which have helped in the preparation of this study and its subsequent revisions. There is not space here to detail all relevant contributions, but I should like to mention my debt to Miss I. M. Walker, of Hamilton Academy; Miss Jessie Buttberg, late of Jordanhill College of Education; Harry Milne, Association of Teachers of Russian; Professor Stanley Nisbet, my predecessor and former mentor at the University of Glasgow; Dan McDade, of Leeds University; and several colleagues in the University of London, notably Professor B. Holmes and J. J. Tomiak of the Institute of Education and Professor E. J. King of King's College. My special thanks are due to Professor A. Nove, of Glasgow University Institute of Soviet and East European Studies, through whose department much of the material was obtained, and his colleagues J. Miller and J. A. Newth, for reading the original manuscript and offering many valuable criticisms and suggestions. I must also thank succeeding generations of students who have provided comment and clarification, and the stimulation to persevere. It goes without saying that responsibility for the use made of any information, for any interpretations made and opinions expressed, is entirely my own.

Edinburgh and Glasgow
May 1978

NIGEL GRANT

ESTONIAN
S.S.R.

LATVIAN
S.S.R.

LITHUANIAN
S.S.R.

R.S.F.S.R.

MOLDAVIAN
S.S.R.

GEORGIAN
S.S.R.

ARMENIAN
S.S.R.

AZERBAIDZHAN
S.S.R.

NORWAY

SWEDEN

FINLAND

POLAND

Leningrad

BYELO-
RUSSIAN
S.S.R.

Moscow

UKRAINIAN
S.S.R.

Kiev

RUSSIAN

TURKEY

IRAQ

IRAN

AFGHANISTAN

KAZAKH
S.S.R.

UZBEK
S.S.R.

TURKMEN S.S.R.

KIRGHIZ
S.S.R.

TADZHIK
S.S.R.

Map of the U.S.S.R

1. Introduction:
The Background to the System

Problems and Handicaps

Few things tell us so much about a country as its schools. In them we can see one of the most important processes of any nation – yesterday's traditions and today's policies moulding and developing the citizens of tomorrow.

It took the Sputnik and its successors to drive home to many people in the West how far the Russians have come in technology from their recent backward state. But the importance of education in the U.S.S.R. goes far beyond rocketry and space navigation; the aim of the Soviet authorities has always been the building of a new kind of society, and they have used the educational system, deliberately and consciously, as a means of attaining this goal. It is, therefore, designed not merely as a machine for the production of scientists, engineers, and technicians, but as an instrument of mass education from which the younger generation gain not only their formal learning, but their social, moral, and political ideas as well. If we want to understand what makes the Soviet Union tick, one of the most profitable ways is to watch what is happening in its schools.

Whether we regard the U.S.S.R. with fear, admiration, or regret, or any mixture of these, we must beware of jumping to conclusions. Educational systems never exist in a vacuum, but are shaped and influenced by the conditions and needs of the societies in which they function. Foreign observers inevitably must pass judgement on what they see, but in doing so they have to avoid making too glib or superficial comparisons with practices and concepts peculiar to their own system. This is particularly true of the Westerner looking at education in the U.S.S.R. Their outlooks are worlds apart, and it is surely futile to apply uncritically to schools in Moscow or Novosibirsk standards more appropriate to London or North Berwick. In the first place, Soviet education is designed for purposes alien to ours, as we shall examine at greater length later. Secondly, the Soviet educational system as it is today was created in the face of handicaps on a scale that it is hard for us in this country to imagine. These drawbacks did much to give the system its present shape, and on that count alone call for our attention. Further, having regard to them should help not only our understanding of Soviet education, but our evaluation of it. Let us therefore take a look at some of the most important of these.

Lands and Peoples

The very geography of the country must have proved something of a hindrance to any régime attempting to achieve universal education. The U.S.S.R. covers an area of nearly nine million square miles, including almost every kind of climatic variation from sub-tropical to polar in its enormous sweep of territory from the deserts of Central Asia to the Arctic, from the Black Sea and the Baltic to the Pacific Ocean. Much of this area is extremely thinly populated, especially in Central Asia and the north. Too much should not be made of purely geographical factors, which should come to matter progressively less as communications continue to improve. But this must have been a much greater handicap in the early days before fast, widespread air transport; and even now there must be difficulties in organizing a school system where the pupils of one school have to come a long way, where distance and weather can interfere with travel and communications, and where extremes of climate and seasonal variations upset what would be regarded elsewhere as the normal routine of the school year. For example, cities like Moscow and Leningrad have little apparent difficulty in getting a reasonable supply of teachers, but things are rather different when schools have to be staffed in areas that lie remote not only from the major cities of the country, but from any kind of town whatever, or where the rigours of climate make normal life more difficult still. The pitiless winter weather is not the only problem; in many places the spring thaw can reduce the countryside to a sea of mud for many weeks. The development of transport has a long way to go before considerations of this kind can be regarded as unimportant.

Another drawback is the size and variety of the population. There are nearly 260 million people in the U.S.S.R., and large numbers alone can be an obstacle to keeping an educational system running smoothly over such a big area. But the issue is further complicated by the variety of nationalities; there are over a hundred of these,[1] each with its own language, customs, and culture. In language alone the picture is one of bewildering complexity: newspapers[2] are published in no less than sixty-five different tongues, some of which have their own distinctive scripts.[3] Of the languages of the fifteen Union Republics, Ukrainian and Byelorussian are certainly close to Russian, but most of them belong to quite different language families. Lithuanian and Latvian belong to the Baltic group, which has some affinity with the Slavonic; Moldavian is a variant of the Rumanian spoken across the border (but is written in the Cyrillic script, like Russian and most of the others); Armenian belongs, with Russian, to the Indo-European family (but so do English, Hindi, and Welsh), and Tadzhik is a form of Persian. The main Central Asian languages – Uzbek, Kazakh, Turkmen, and Kirgiz, plus Azerbaidzhani in Transcaucasia – are of the same family as Turkish, while Estonian is closely related to Finnish. As for the Georgian language in the Caucasus, with its indigenous script and ancient literature, this has no known relationship to any major group.

Further, many of the Union Republics contain sizeable minorities within their own boundaries, such as the Abkhazians and South Ossetians in Georgia or the Nakhichevan and Nagorny Karabakh peoples in Azerbaidzhan. In the R.S.F.S.R. (the Russian Federation, the major Union Republic) there is a veritable patchwork quilt of nationalities – Finnic peoples such as the Karelians, Komi, Mansi, Khanty, and Nanai; Turko-Tatar peoples such as the Kalmyks, Chuvash, Bashkir, Yakuti, and

Tatars; peoples of the Far East like the Tungus, Lamut, Koryak, Chukchi, and many others, mostly small in numbers and widely scattered. These minorities are variously organized into 'Autonomous Soviet Socialist Republics' (A.S.S.R.), 'Autonomous Regions', or 'National Areas' within the larger units of the Union Republics. While some of the minority groups are very small – several, like the Yukagir and the Aleuts, number only a few hundreds – others are quite substantial. There are nearly as many Ukrainians as there are Frenchmen, for example; and two other peoples (the Uzbeks and the Byelorussians) have over nine millions each. The other peoples of the Union Republics range from one to six million; there are nearly six million Tatars, and other groups, like the Chuvash, Mordva, Bashkirs, Poles, Jews, and Germans, number well over a million each. The Russian language, though more widely spoken than any other and used as the official language of the Russian Federation and the U.S.S.R., is the mother tongue of barely half the population.[4]

This mixture of peoples and babel of tongues would create problems for any educational system, especially one so closely controlled from the centre. One possible solution would have been to press ahead with the overt and deliberate Russification of the whole country, but this was rejected by the Soviet government right from the beginning, and Stalin's slogan 'a culture national in form and socialist in content' set the seal of official approval on a policy of pluralism. The Constitution of the U.S.S.R.[5] has a great deal to say about racial equality; racial or national discrimination is declared to be an offence punishable by law (Article 36), and the use of the native tongue is guaranteed in the lawcourts, Soviets, and the like, in all the Union Republics and their subdivisions; Article 45 insists on 'the opportunity to attend a school where teaching is in the native language'. It is well known that on many matters the Constitution says one thing while something quite different is practised, but in this case, on the whole, the provisions do appear to be carried into effect. In principle, children do have the opportunity of being taught in their own languages at school, and in some places at university level as well.

In practice, however, there are limitations. Complete instruction at all stages is available in Russian, in the languages of the other fourteen Union Republics, and (within the R.S.F.S.R.) in Tatar and Bashkir; but among the minorities of intermediate size, schooling in the native tongue is given only up to the eighth class (about age fifteen), and among the smaller groups only up to the fourth class (age eleven), all instruction thereafter being in Russian. Among the tiny nationalities of the Far North and Far East, the first two classes only are taught in the vernacular, always supposing a written vernacular exists; otherwise, Russian has to be used from the start. Whatever the Constitution may say, numbers of speakers, and in some cases the level of development of the languages, impose practical restrictions on their use.

But there are further complications, since Russian, as the official language of the Soviet Union, has to be learned as well. In some Republics, such as Georgia, where special pains are taken to foster the ancient language and culture, pupils stay one year longer at school than their Russian counterparts; but in areas where there has been a significant degree of Russian settlement (notably in Kazakhstan), or of Russian cultural penetration (as in the cities of the Ukraine), the Russian language tends to gain ground at the expense of the vernacular. The existence of minorities within minorities complicates things even further, as does the inclusion of a foreign language in all school curricula. Thus, attempts to cater for the needs of the various national groups, while also trying to educate them as citizens of the Soviet Union as a whole, may produce additional burdens and tensions.

Variety and confusion apart, the prospect facing the Soviet authorities after the revolution was distinctly unpromising. The Russian Empire was backward in education as in most things. Literacy, which can be taken as a fair guide to a nation's minimum educational level, has been variously estimated, but was probably not much above thirty per cent over the entire country. In European Russia, things were rather better; living standards were higher, the population was more Westernized than elsewhere, and the innovations of Peter the Great and others had borne some fruit. In spite of many black spots, where the masses of the peasantry were termed 'dark' or benighted, there had been enough voluntary effort to raise literacy west of the Urals and the Volga to about forty per cent over the whole area – much less in the countryside, but higher in the towns. Schooling in the major cities could, at its best, bear comparison with that of the highest quality in Europe, but this was available only to a small minority. Generally, the educational picture in Western Russia was extremely patchy, and on the whole lagged well behind most of Central and Western Europe.

In the Asian and Northern areas, however, the situation was appalling. Most of the Arctic peoples still lived in Stone Age conditions. In 1914, Tadzhikistan had ten elementary schools, thirteen teachers, and a literacy rate of one half of one per cent; Turkmenia had fifty-eight schools, literacy reaching the level of 0.7 per cent; of the population of Uzbekistan, which includes such ancient cities as Tashkent, Bukhara, and Samarkand, only two per cent were literate; in Georgia, for all its relative prosperity and ancient culture, only twenty per cent of the people were able to read and write. As for Kirgizia, it was in an even worse plight; it had to start from nothing, lacking even a written language. In the other Eastern parts of the Empire the picture was much the same,[6] bearing more resemblance to the rest of the land-mass of Asia than to the European part of the country.

This legacy of backwardness would have been bad enough for any government, let alone one as ambitious as the Soviet; but the birth-pangs of the revolution and the havoc of war served to make things even worse.

Revolution and War

The Soviet Union came into being after three years of war had exhausted Russia, thrown her into the convulsions of the revolution of 1917, and shorn her of vast tracts of her richest land at the humiliating Treaty of Brest-Litovsk. But worse was still to come; even before the Germans were forced to withdraw from the

Ukraine in 1918, civil war broke out. It went on steadily until 1921, and was not completely over until the following year. During that time the Red and White armies fought it out on several fronts throughout the country, while several foreign nations, including Britain, France, the U.S.A., Poland, Japan, and an army of expatriate Czechoslovaks, intervened in the struggle. Hostilities between the intervening powers and the Soviet government were confused and spasmodic, punctuated by uneasy truces and ambiguous diplomatic overtures. The conflict was sometimes direct and open, sometimes taking the form of military and financial aid to approved régimes by the Allies. The position was further complicated by several nations entering or quitting the war as policy or special interest dictated. But during much of this time the Soviet government was fighting for its existence, and the war between the Reds and the Whites went on, with great ruthlessness on both sides, to the bitter end. When the dust settled, the Soviet authorities found themselves in power in a country that had been pushed even farther back into poverty and backwardness.

The destruction of life and property had been enormous (to say nothing of the legacy of mistrust that survives today). Nor was it just a question of war devastation, battle casualties, or the loss of those who fell victim to terror and counter-terror; many regions had undergone several changes of régime, Red and White, and in this general atmosphere of political and social upheaval, of anxiety and uncertainty about the future, any attempt to come seriously to grips with the deep-seated educational problems was well-nigh impossible. This had to wait for more settled conditions, and was still bound to be a slow process. As late as 1926, forty-two per cent were still illiterate in European Russia (which contained the bulk of the population); the minority areas were much worse – in Azerbaidzhan, for example, the figure was seventy-five per cent.[7] Even in something as fundamental as literacy, the surface of the problem had barely been scratched.

In the years that followed, the difficulties in the way of educating the entire nation were obvious enough. At the same time, they were a constant reminder of the need for action, if the aim of the Soviet government was to be realized. The task of building from the ruins of the Russian Empire a modern, industrial, and socialist society was pushed on with a ruthlessness – and at a human cost – that is well known. But no measure of ruthless determination could in itself be enough; for the success of such projects as the Five Year Plans, the authorities depended on educational development no less than on the mustering of man-power and economic resources. There had to be a new force of engineers, scientists, technicians of all kinds. The upheavals of the revolution had thinned the ranks of the Russian intelligentsia, which had to be reinforced and expanded. Industrial develop-ment needed more skilled workers of all kinds. No possible source of talent could be left untapped, and the only way of meeting these needs was by the rapid development of a planned system of mass education. The building of the Soviet society also demanded the energetic propagation of communist ideas, and the schools were used for this too – directly as vehicles for the teach-ing of loyalty to the régime, and indirectly in providing the liter-acy necessary for the dissemination of propaganda by newspaper, broadsheet, and poster.

The drive towards industrialization was, therefore, accom-panied by determined efforts to extend and improve the school system at all levels. The needs of the developing Soviet society were regarded as paramount. During the 1920s there had been a surge of experimentation in education; John Dewey's activity and project methods, the Dalton assignment plan, Western 'pro-gressive' techniques of all kinds found their way into the Soviet schools. But this did not last for long; the needs of the national economy, the call for ever-increasing efficiency, and the general tightening-up of society at large brought in a reaction. By the 1930s a halt had been called to what were described, rather un-justly, as 'irresponsible experiments' in the schools, and the Stalin era reimposed a strict routine of examinations, formal teaching, and strict classroom discipline on the traditional Continental model. This involved the reintroduction of many features of pre-revolutionary schooling, but was applied on a mass scale and geared to the political needs of the Soviet state and the Communist Party. By 1939 the literacy rate had risen to eighty-one per cent, and the production of specialists and skilled personnel was increasing rapidly.

Then, in 1941, Hitler's armies invaded the U.S.S.R., striking deep into the country to the very outskirts of Moscow and Leningrad, to the Volga and the Caucasus, before they were finally driven out. Great areas in the west were devastated, including most of the Ukraine and much of European Russia. Loss of life has been estimated at over 35 millions, military and civil, including deaths from starvation and disease. Quite apart from the dislocation caused, the loss of teachers, and the diversion of resources to the war effort, 82,000 schools were totally destroyed – a loss to the country of 15 million school places.

In spite of the original handicaps in 1917, however, and in the face of massive setbacks like the Second World War, much has been accomplished. Literacy is now virtually universal. (So it is claimed by Soviet and U.N.E.S.C.O. figures; some commentators have suggested that there may be as much as five to ten per cent residual illiteracy, but even if this figure were accepted it would not be large in the circumstances.) There has been a spectacular rise in educational provision at all levels from nursery to university. Ten-year schooling is now free and compulsory from seven to seventeen, and although there is evidence of unofficial drop-out in some remote areas (and occasionally nearer the main centres of population), practically everybody now attends the common course up to age fifteen, and the great majority study further, in one way or another, for at least two years beyond that. Even before compulsory school, the bulk of the age-group experience at least two years of kindergarten, and at the other end of the process, the number of students in higher education has grown to nearly forty times the pre-revolutionary figure; and judging from the standard of scientific work, Soviet higher education and research can readily stand comparison with that of the West. At a time when the importance of education as a life-long process is growing more apparent, the numbers of students engaged in further training or courses for the raising of qualifications is especially noteworthy. There are now over thirty-four millions of these – well over fifty times the pre-revolutionary level.[8]

By any standards an achievement on this scale in little over sixty years would be impressive enough. When we remember that with the losses and destruction of war the time was in effect very much shorter, we can see that whatever reservations we may have about many features of the educational system, it commands our closest attention.

It will be seen later that rigidity and central control is an outstanding feature of education in the U.S.S.R. This is due in part to its being guided to political ends, in part to the fact that the revolution inherited a long-standing centralizing tradition. Tsarist Russia had an extensive system of schools run by voluntary bodies, which was not centrally controlled. However, the official system was, and it was from this that Soviet education grew. To expect the individual stress that we in this country claim as a central characteristic of our system would be unrealistic – prescription from the centre followed automatically. It is doubtless true that this suited the Soviet leaders well enough, and they certainly made use of it, but it was not their invention. Useful to the communist régime though it was, tight centralization had its origins in the habits and traditions of Tsarist Russia. Revolutions have a tendency to take their colour from the powers they overthrow.

To those accustomed to the comparative freedom and flexibility of the school systems in Britain, the centralization and uniformity of the Soviet system seems undesirable, even repellent (though it would seem less remarkable to a teacher or pupil in France). But the situations are not comparable; our pattern of gradual reform (with periods of marking time) would have made little impression on problems as great as those facing the U.S.S.R. When all the circumstances are considered, it is extremely doubtful if such spectacular advances could have been made in any other way.

Education and Ideology

Education in the U.S.S.R. is primarily a political tool for the construction of a communist society. It has of course other purposes and other effects, but these are of secondary importance; from the first decrees on education after the October Revolution up to the present, educational policy has always been conceived in the light of social and political objectives, to which all other considerations must be subordinate. 'Without teaching there is no knowledge,' Lenin once remarked, 'and without knowledge there is no communism.' In 1958, during a major overhaul of the school system, the Central Committee of the Communist Party spelled out the attitudes that the schools were expected to promulgate:

Upbringing must inculcate in the schoolchildren a love of knowledge and of work, and respect for people who work; it must shape the communist world outlook of the pupils and rear them in the spirit of communist morality and of boundless loyalty to the country and the people, and in the spirit of proletarian internationalism.[9]

The Basic Law on Education, brought into effect in 1974, summed up the objectives of the system thus:

The goal of public education in the U.S.S.R. is the preparation of highly educated, well-rounded, physically healthy and active builders of communist society, brought up on the ideas of Marxism–Leninism and in the spirit of respect for Soviet laws and socialist legality, capable of working successfully in various areas of socio-economic cultural construction, actively participating in social and state activity, and ready to defend selflessly the socialist homeland and to preserve and increase its material and spiritual wealth and protect and preserve nature. Public education in the U.S.S.R. is called upon to ensure the development and satisfaction of the spiritual and intellectual needs of Soviet man.[10]

What emerges from the often turgid prose of official statements is that the skills, knowledge, and attitudes imparted in the schools are determined by the needs of Soviet society in a conscious and deliberate way. Soviet society needs an ever-improved and ever-expanding skilled labour force; consequently vocational training and guidance are expanded. Soviet society (like all expanding industrial societies) needs a high degree of literacy and general culture; therefore the schools strive to impart universal competence in the basic skills and whet the children's cultural appetites, helped by the traditional Russian veneration for learning and the arts. Further, Soviet society (or its leaders) requires 'political awareness' in the mass of the population. This is more than mere conformity, which usually comes more easily through ignorance. Dumb acquiescence will not do; what is wanted is conformity based on knowledge and study of political theory, conformity in the positive sense. The educational system accordingly seeks to put over the political attitudes of the Communist Party and the theories of Marxism–Leninism. It does not seem to have had much success in obtaining widespread understanding of political theory, judging by the frequency of official complaints; but it has managed to instil a high degree of loyalty, in public at any rate, to the régime.

Not only do the Soviet authorities openly declare the political aims of their educational system, they deny emphatically that it could or should be otherwise. From the Soviet standpoint the basic issue is simple, leaving aside the emotional overtones of words like 'indoctrination' and 'propaganda', which they regard as irrelevant. They take the view that education must function according to the needs of society, and that theirs is by definition a socialist society moving towards communism, a society which needs trained citizens who will all be able – and willing – to continue with the job of social transformation. Education must therefore be political in nature, since this is a political task. As Khrushchov put it at the twenty-first Congress of the Communist Party of the Soviet Union, 'To arrive at communism, that most fair and perfect society . . . we must start right now educating the man of the future.'

As for the claims of other systems to be non-political in aim, they are dismissed, in Lenin's words, as 'hypocrisy and lies'. Most non-communist countries teach religion in their schools, that is, they indoctrinate the pupils with a particular world outlook; also, they might add, national traditions and patriotic attitudes are taught everywhere, openly or covertly. In the Soviet view, their own kind of indoctrination is franker, more thorough, and embraces a wider field of teaching than that of other systems, but they would deny that the process of indoctrination itself is a monopoly of the communist approach to education.

Widespread and thorough it certainly is. Directly and indirectly, the communist viewpoint is put over at every stage of schooling, and reinforced by the other media of communication outside the schools, such as the theatre, films, radio, television, and the Press, while the youth organizations act as a link between the school and the world outside.

Direct systematic instruction in political doctrine is not greatly in evidence in the programmes of the younger classes in the schools, though older children have a course of 'Social Studies' (*Obshchestvovedenie*), a fairly extensive study of the various aspects of Marxist–Leninist theory.[11] In higher education, however, it plays a big part; all students, whatever they are studying and whatever kind of institute they attend, must attend classes in philosophy and theory of history, the history of the Communist Party of the Soviet Union, and the principles of political economy (all from the Marxist standpoint, of course). They must also pass examinations in these subjects, which take up a minor yet substantial part of their curricular time; indeed, trainee teachers spend a higher proportion of their time on these courses than they do on teaching methods, psychology, and educational theory put together. Thus it is ensured that all graduates emerge from their courses not only as highly trained specialists but, in theory at least, briefed in communist theories and ideas.

Throughout the rest of the educational system, the curriculum is saturated with Soviet principles. All subjects, wherever possible, are presented from the Marxist point of view and used to make political points. Literature and history lend themselves readily to this treatment, while in geography and language much can be done through the judicious selection of reading material. The sciences and the fine arts can be pressed into service here too, but in this area the authorities have been soft-pedalling since the death of Stalin; the influence of Lysenko in genetics and Zhdanov in the creative arts, for all the resultant orthodoxy, also produced a creative sterility that the U.S.S.R. could ill afford. The easing off, however, has been only relative, not absolute, and Party control has been sharply reasserted from time to time when it has been felt that liberalization has gone too far. Even when 'dogmatism' is most scathingly condemned, the authorities still maintain the principle that there is an ideologically 'correct' approach to every field of knowledge and study. Moral education too is presented on the basis of comradeship, loyalty to the group, and understanding of the duties and responsibilities of the Soviet citizen. Even in sport and physical education the point is constantly made that physical fitness is a duty of the future builder of communism, to enable him to work better for the good of the community.

Such close links between curriculum and political theory tend, of course, to put inquiry into a straitjacket, an inherent danger in all organized creeds, political or otherwise. It also increases the headaches of school administrators, officials, and teachers; political lines change, sometimes abruptly, and when they do they bring in their wake considerable upheavals at school level. During the heyday of Stalin's ascendancy, the 'cult of personality' was closely reflected in textbooks and lessons throughout the country. When Stalin was posthumously toppled from his pedestal, the new line of policy led to drastic revisions in the material used in the schools. In 1956, for example, there were no history examinations for final-year school pupils, the old textbook having been withdrawn and the new still in the course of preparation. The gap was filled partly by teaching without a text, but not sufficiently to make a uniform examination possible. For the same reason, the teaching of literature was temporarily curtailed farther down the school while revision of texts was being carried out. Changes of policy, even fairly minor ones, keep the textbook writers busy; the Soviet schools seem to be full of brand-new books, especially for such potentially thorny subjects as the history of the U.S.S.R. This is possibly also one reason for the stress on refresher courses for teachers.

In extra-curricular activities too, political content is prominent. Slogans, posters, wall-newspapers, statues, and portraits of leaders meet the eye everywhere in the schools. Slogans and poster themes may be directly political, such as 'Forward to the building of communism' or 'We must study and work as Lenin taught'; or patriotic, such as 'Glory to the Soviet people – a people of heroes!' There are many which exhort children to study hard and be a credit to the community, others which blazon protestations of peace and friendship over the school walls. A favourite theme, variously illustrated, is *'Miru mir!'* – 'Peace to the world!', a play on words arising from the fact that the Russian word *mir* means either 'world' or 'peace'. Portraits of Brezhnev are frequently seen (sometimes flanked by other leaders), far more than were those of Khrushchov in his time, but still with nothing approaching the ubiquity of Stalin before the Twentieth Congress. Lenin, however, is everywhere, in a great variety of pictures showing him speaking, writing, pondering, patting children on the head, pointing dramatically into the future, or just looking out from a wall swathed in red drapery. Many schools have a room or hall 'dedicated to Lenin' which they use for meetings and displays; Leningrad School No. 290, for example, has in its Lenin Hall exhibits of photographs illustrating the life of Lenin, representations of Lenin in the theatre and the cinema, together with letters and messages from actors who had played the part. Busts, full-size statues, and plaques bearing his utterances abound. This reached a peak of intensity during the 1970 celebrations of the centenary of Lenin's birth, but was and remains common. In the classroom and out of it, the Soviet schoolchild is never far from reminders of the ideas and aims of the régime and its founder.

In many countries, including our own, there is some degree of conflict between the influence of the school and that of outside agencies, such as television. In the U.S.S.R. this is not the case; since the media of mass communication are just as subject as the schools to control by government and Party, they reinforce what is taught in the classroom instead of clashing with it. Much labour and money is lavished on the theatre, films, papers, museums, and the like, particular attention being paid to young people. The authorities go so far as to run hundreds of special children's theatres, cinemas, cultural centres, and camps, and, through the youth organizations, newspapers as well. The youth movements' functions, as we shall see, are not purely political, especially the sections for younger children (the Pioneers), but in their job of attending to various leisure activities they contrive to convey the political message incidentally, by methods much the same as those of the schools themselves. By their close links with the schools, the organizations become in effect a branch of the educational system. The children, in their leisure as in their work, are thus kept close to the social and political influences considered suitable by the Soviet régime.

One aspect of this orientation of education is the attitude taken towards religion. Official policy in the U.S.S.R. has always been hostile towards religion, and has been put into effect by devices ranging from almost complete proscription to bare tolerance combined with anti-religious propaganda of varying degrees of virulence. This is partly for ideological reasons. Marxist theory regards all supernatural religion as 'opium of the people', a device to distract the masses from the problems of this world by getting them to concentrate on hopes of better things in the next. Theory seemed to be confirmed in practice by the behaviour of the Russian Orthodox Church. Revolutionaries saw the Church as a heavily committed ally of Tsarism, acting as a 'spiritual cloak for the landlords' as one of them put it. Also, when the revolution broke out the official leadership of the Church, under Patriarch Tikhon, took sides against the Soviet government, doing anything within its very limited power towards its overthrow. Since the Church had thus let itself be identified not only with reaction in the past but with counter-revolution and intervention in the present, the anti-religious reaction was perhaps inevitable, even without Marxist theory to back it up.

The churches in the Soviet Union have had their ups and downs since then. During the Second World War there was an increase in toleration, to which the religious leaders responded by throwing the weight of their patriotic exhortations into the war effort. At the present time, the position is roughly a combination of toleration and official discouragement; the Constitution (Article 52) states that 'Freedom of religious worship and freedom of anti-religious propaganda is recognized for all citizens'. Freedom of pro-religious propaganda is not mentioned, and though religious observances take place quite freely, at least in the major cities, there are still many indirect pressures, and adherence to any church is likely to be a considerable drawback to the ambitious. From time to time, if church-going appears to be on the increase, anti-religious propaganda is stepped up in the Press and the schools. As far as religious education is concerned, this is completely divorced from the classroom; apart from a few church-run seminaries for the training of priests, education and religion never come together. The aforementioned article of the Constitution declares the separation of state and church, church and school. Religious instruction is therefore not given in the schools at all, and parents who want it must make their own individual arrangements through their own churches in their own time.

The values and attitudes that pervade Soviet education are not to be explained by Marxism–Leninism alone. For all its insistence on looking to the future and its stress on 'proletarian internationalism', the system has strong roots in the traditions of the Russian Empire. 'Soviet patriotism' is not only 'love of the socialist motherland' – it contains a strong tinge of straight Russian nationalism as well. National consciousness, once suspect as a bourgeois phenomenon, is now respectable. The Second World War is referred to as 'The Great Patriotic War'. Geographical atlases bear titles like 'Our Motherland' (*nasha rodina* has much stronger emotional overtones than its English translation), and such phrases as 'our country' are liberally sprinkled through the history books. Although any comparisons drawn between the old régime and the new are inevitably flattering to the Soviet era, great emphasis is laid on certain 'positive' achievements of the past, and on the virtues of the Russian people in general. In the teaching of history and literature, national heroes are very much to the fore; Pushkin and Chekhov, Mussorgsky and Tchaikovsky lead a galaxy of stars venerated for their services to the arts in Russia; Peter the Great and Alexander I, among many other princes, make up for their ideological failings by their contributions to the wellbeing, influence, and power of Russia in the past. In the sciences, past achievements (real or claimed) of Russian inventors are played up to an extent that often causes a good deal of amusement in the West. Far from despising national sentiment, the Soviet authorities use it as a prop for securing further loyalty to the régime, with considerable success. Some observers [12] have suggested that the high degree of commitment among young people is due more to patriotic pride than to doctrinal conviction.

It is this political direction of the Soviet educational system that gives it its special character and largely determines its form. Details of school administration, organization, and curriculum have changed, often radically, in the years since the revolution, but the salient features have remained constant throughout: it has always been a *mass* system and a *planned* system, subject to political control and closely supervised.

The mass character of Soviet education is, clearly, a reflection of its social aims. These would be unattainable if education were regarded as an obstacle race or a sieve for catching the most able and discarding the rest. A highly selective system might conceivably produce the required intelligentsia and specialists, though even this is doubtful – in an industrial society there has to be a large number of technicians for every technologist, and a host of skilled workers for every technician, if their work is to be at all effective. Consequently education has to raise the entire population to as high a level as possible, or the training of specialists is bound to prove futile in practice. Hence the unremitting assault on illiteracy throughout the Soviet period, and the continual efforts to raise the 'cultural level' of the people through the schools, mass communications, and every other method that could be pressed into service.

The Soviet régime, as we have seen, aims higher than mere passive acquiescence, so that for positive political commitment among the masses, mass education is again imperative. 'An illiterate person,' Lenin remarked, 'stands outside; he must first be taught the ABC. Without this, there can be no politics; without this, there are only rumours, gossip, tales, prejudices, but no politics.' Literacy and the highest development of general education are thus regarded as a political necessity for the government and a civic duty for the individual. It is for this reason that although much has been done in the field of vocational and specialist education, the authorities – and, to all appearances, public opinion – insist on the system's retaining its mass character. Reforms may bring in more diverse courses for senior pupils, special schools may cater for artists and ballet dancers, but underlying the variations is the stress on providing a basic general education, covering the same ground and on the same terms for all, regardless of background or future occupation. A more diversified and selective system would be regarded with grave suspicion as a barrier to the realization of the political aims of Soviet education, even if it were scholastically more efficient.

A system closely tied to the needs of a developing society must inevitably be carefully planned and coordinated. The Russian intellectual tradition and Marxist theory alike have a horror of improvisation and 'muddling through'. The result is a vast organizational network throughout the country, in education as in other branches of national life; and though complaints of bureaucratic inefficiency and red tape are often heard (more frequently in recent years), it is unlikely that planning as such would be seriously challenged in the U.S.S.R., even by the most severe critics of the particular handling of some particular plan. All aspects of Soviet education are, therefore, planned in detail, from the finance of universities to the curriculum and teaching methods for the elementary classes, from building programmes to admission figures for the colleges. The working of the plans, though some of the details are delegated to local bodies, is watched over by the Union and Republican Ministries of Education. Organization as well as policy is also under the eye of the Communist Party, locally and nationally. Thus the working of the system is controlled every step of the way.

In principle, then, anything we observe in the Soviet schools has been consciously planned for the purpose of running a system of mass education designed for the rearing of the 'new man' and the building of a communist society. Of course, it does not always work out like that in practice. Central directives are not always carried out, unauthorized practices may continue in the schools. Indeed, difficulty of implementation of policy is something of a general problem, especially in the countryside. But unofficial practices, whether negative or positive, are regarded as a failing, not a virtue. For us, living in a society where so many features of the educational system owe their existence to use and wont rather than any deliberate policy, it is important to bear this in mind when taking a look at what actually happens in the U.S.S.R.

2. The Educational System: General Characteristics (Part One)

Central Control

One of the most prominent features of Soviet education, which highlights its differences from other large-scale systems of mass education, is the extent of tight control exercised by the central authorities, and the degree of uniformity enforced in principle and practice through the length and breadth of the Soviet Union. In such a vast and varied country there are naturally some local differences, and there are also plenty of instances of things happening at school level without the knowledge or approval of the higher authorities; given the extent and complexity of the chain of command, it could hardly be otherwise. In the formulation of basic policy, however, and to a considerable extent in the details of school practice, the authorities in Moscow keep a firm grip on what happens in schools and colleges from Riga to Vladivostok.

The reasons for this concentration of power in a few hands are not far to seek. In the years immediately following the revolution, the need for quick results in education was so desperate and obvious that techniques of gradualism and *laissez faire* were out of the question if anything was to be done at all. The crying need, as we have seen, was for mobilization of all resources, which meant that planning was a must; this in turn meant careful coordination, hence the high degree of central control that still exists. Nor was this in any way remarkable at the time; the habit of prescription from the top was so deeply engrained in the traditional Russian ways of thinking that it can be doubted if devolution and decentralization were ever seriously considered. Further, this fitted (and still fits) the single-mindedness of Soviet educational aims. Education, in the official view, must serve the needs, political and otherwise, of Soviet society, as interpreted by the Communist Party. If the system is to reflect closely enough the development and shifts of government policy, it has to be kept firmly in the hands of the political authorities. From time to time there have been changes of detail, some matters being left to local bodies to work out more specifically; but the basic assumption that the bulk of policy-making, and the residue of power, should rest in the keeping of the central authorities, has never been seriously challenged. Any departure from this principle would be stigmatized as nothing better than anarchy.

There is, however, no single ministry responsible for the entire educational system of the U.S.S.R. Even at the highest level, control seems diffuse. Responsibility for the general schools, for teacher training, and educational research rests with the all-Union Ministry of Education, while the all-Union Ministry of Higher and Secondary Specialized Education takes care of the universities and most of the colleges and secondary specialized schools. Other bodies, such as the Ministries of Public Health, Agriculture, etc., are involved in the running of specialized colleges and schools, and the Ministry of Culture deals with matters that might be termed educational in the less formal sense. Schools for the training of skilled workers are the responsibility of the Committee of the Council of Ministers for Vocational-Technical Education.

The pattern is duplicated, with some variations, at the level of the Union Republics. There are in addition twenty 'Autonomous Republics' with Ministries of Education (not of Higher Education) of their own; most of these are inside the Russian Federation (the R.S.F.S.R.). Thus, decisions affecting the general schools are passed from the U.S.S.R. Ministry of Education through no less than thirty-five ministries. Most of the details for the translation of policy into action are worked out by the Union Ministry, in conjunction with the Academy of Pedagogic Sciences, and are passed on to the republic ministries for implementation. Officially, there are channels to be gone through in the form of the Supreme Soviets and the Councils of Ministers of the constituent republics, but in practice this is not very different from direct instruction.

The ministries of the Union Republics make such changes as local conditions demand, usually minor variations with the approval of the central authorities. (The ministries of the Autonomous Republics do the same, though their area of discretion is less.) From ministerial level instructions are passed on to regional, provincial and city departments of education, then to district departments, and finally to school directors and teachers. The farther down the chain one goes, the greater is the amount of detail laid down for the conduct of the schools. By the time it comes to the teacher, the area of personal discretion, though greater than it used to be, is very small. Not only basic policy, but the content of the curriculum, schemes of work, textbooks, teaching methods, and the like are prescribed for the teacher in considerable detail.

Surprisingly, there was not even a Union Ministry of Education until the mid-1960s. There were the central Ministries of Higher Education, Culture, and the like, but the highest ministries for the running of the general schools were to be found only at republic level. In practice, this made little difference. For one thing, the republic ministries tended to follow the lead of the largest and most influential, that of the R.S.F.S.R. For another, ministries are in any case not the fountain-heads of policy or legislation. State power lies, in theory, with the Supreme Soviet of the U.S.S.R.; when it is not in session, which is most of the time, the Council of Ministers exercises power on its behalf. This in turn is effectively controlled by the central organs of the Communist Party of the Soviet Union, the real source of power in education as in other things. It is therefore of minor importance whether the ministries are centralized or not; the Party is.

Major decisions of policy, then, are made by the central Party organs, often after trying out the ideas first by flying kites in the form of debates in the Press or discussions at meetings, thereby gaining some idea of the state of opinion on the matter in hand. The decisions are then passed on to the Supreme Soviet – a theoretically necessary but purely formal step – and become law. The Council of Ministers then passes them on to the appropriate ministries, and so on down the line. When an all-Union Ministry of Education was eventually set up in the middle of 1966, this was an important administrative convenience, but did not reflect any fundamental change in the structure of power; the system was, in effect, centralized already, a situation which the creation of the new ministry formalized but did not create.

One result of this system is a high degree of uniformity all over the country. Whether as a result of direction or emulation, schools, textbooks, curricula, and teaching methods are closely similar throughout the U.S.S.R. With a few differences, children in, say, the fifth form in an eight-year school in places as far apart as Moscow and Magnitogorsk, Tashkent and Tallinn, wear the same uniforms, observe the same rules of behaviour, and study the same subjects from the same textbooks at the same pace. When they complete the basic course at the age of fifteen, the alternatives available for the next stage of their education are substantially the same wherever they may be.

There are some variations, of course, official and otherwise. The main difference is one of language; similar though they may be in other respects, the native-language schools in Tashkent or Tbilisi will give instruction in Uzbek or Georgian rather than in Russian. (There is a parallel system of Russian-medium schools in many non-Russian areas.) This in turn often leads to other changes because of the extra burden of learning Russian as well; in Georgia (an extreme case) children stay at school a year longer than their Russian counterparts largely for this reason. There are also minor differences in textbooks and curricula from one republic to another. Textbooks in the non-Russian republics are usually straight translations of those in use in the R.S.F.S.R., but not infrequently the republics have their own when local conditions make this necessary, as with the treatment of local history, for example. Further, official policy encourages the national cultures of the several minorities, so that such subjects as art, music, literature, and the like are presented with strong bias towards the national idiom. Even if the sciences are similarly taught throughout the country, then, singing and painting are liable to vary strikingly from place to place.

Even within the republics further variations can be found. All schools teach one foreign language to all their pupils, but the languages offered vary. Most schools teach English or German, with French and Spanish lagging behind in popularity.[1] Again, although the normal practice is to begin a foreign language at the age of twelve or thereabouts, there is an increasing number of schools where it starts at the age of eight, the language being used as soon as possible as the medium of instruction in other subjects.* Most schools are day schools, but boarding schools and 'extended day schools' exist alongside them. There are also certain special schools, pilot schemes, experimental schools, and other variants all over the country. Generally, the picture of Soviet schooling is not quite as uniform as it might appear at first.

Nonetheless, these variations, though real, are minor – the basic curriculum and the basic aims of education remain pretty constant throughout. Also, the aforementioned variations are there at the behest of the central authorities, not because someone at local level has been showing some initiative and originality in trying out new ideas. In the case of pilot schemes, they are frequently set up in a few places by the central authorities in order to try out something before deciding whether to apply it to the system as a whole. When eight-year schooling was introduced in 1958, for instance, the programme had already been tested in fifty selected schools in the R.S.F.S.R. from September 1957. Similarly, when major modifications were made in the school curriculum in 1966, they had already been worked out experimentally by the Academy of Pedagogical Sciences, with pilot projects in selected schools, since the beginning of the 1964 school year.

From the point of view of the individual child, there are ways in which he can vary his own course of study to some extent. Subjects cannot be dropped, but senior pupils now have much more time for options than was the case in the 1950s and the early 1960s – rising to four hours a week in the last two years. But it is

* See pp. 90–91

possible for a child to *add* to his curriculum outside school hours through the 'circles' or clubs run by the youth organizations. Except where the school still works in shifts, afternoons are mostly free; if he can find a few others similarly inclined, the pupil may study another language or more art or music or anything else from a wide range of activities in this extra time, either in the school or at a Pioneer Palace or Centre. But this is an extra. The basic programme of the school remains substantially uniform for all.

Unofficially, too, there are some breaks in the picture of nation-wide sameness. Evasions of regulations are under constant fire in the educational Press, which implies that they are common. Old methods of teaching languages, for instance, prove difficult to legislate out of existence; there is evidence that in some of the more remote areas the full teaching programmes are not always realized because of shortage of adequate facilities; the maximum size of classes tends to be a hope rather than a reality; official standards of building maintenance are not always observed; there are even cases of children being allowed to leave school and take jobs at the age of fourteen or less, although the legal leaving age is fifteen. In education as in general living standards, there is still a marked disparity between town and country. Country schools are usually much worse off than city schools for buildings, equipment, and supply of teachers; communications are often difficult, and supplies are liable to be delayed. Further, the choice of educational facilities, perhaps inevitably, is much more limited in the countryside – where, it should be remembered, half the population of the U.S.S.R. still lives. A great deal has yet to be done before the peasant's child can hope to have educational opportunities on a par with the child of the urban worker. This is, perhaps, their greatest single problem.[2]

Just how big the gap is between theory and practice is almost impossible for the observer to judge, beyond noting reports and complaints in the Soviet Press. It is clear, however, that most variations from the set pattern exist because the central authorities do not always manage to have their edicts translated into practice, and that whenever possible they are brought into line.

Departures from the pattern laid down by the central authorities, then, may exist with official approval, such as language differences or experimental schools. Sometimes they are unofficial (as when local bodies fail to comply with central directives) and are liable to attack when discovered. Sometimes, again, the central authorities may know that regulations are not being observed, but are unable to do much about it because of lack of facilities, shortage of personnel, or because fulfilment of the educational plans might throw the economy of the area out of gear. (For example, the services of youths who should, strictly speaking, still be at school may be urgently needed to get the harvest in.) Finally, some details of curriculum and school organization are sometimes left to the discretion of the local authorities. But voluntary relinquishing of authority is rare.

For all the local differences in the Soviet system, the general picture by British or American standards is one of substantial uniformity throughout the country, with the central authority, acting through the various levels of the Communist Party, seeking to keep its finger on everything that happens from the office of a ministry of education to the classroom of an elementary teacher. For this reason it is possible to generalize about Soviet education more easily and accurately than about any other country of anything approaching the size and complexity of the U.S.S.R.

Science and Technology

'No society,' says George Counts, the American educationist, 'has ever committed itself so unreservedly in words to the mastery and development of mathematics and the natural sciences.' Certainly one of the things that strike the British observer about Soviet education is the continual stress on science and the scientific method. Whereas there is still a tendency in our schools to talk about 'science' as if it were a single subject like history, literature, or languages, and treat it as of interest mainly to the potential specialist, the Soviet schools give a prominent place to the various branches of science and technology, not just with an eye to the needs of the army of specialists being assiduously trained at the present time, but also as a fundamental part of the general education of all pupils, whether they intend to specialize in that side or not.

In higher education, there is a much greater bias towards the scientific and technological side than there is in this country, and particularly towards the applied sciences such as engineering, agronomy, industrial chemistry. While the absolute number of students is rising all the time, the proportion of scientific specialists is rising even faster. This stress may seem even heavier than it is, since the Russian word *nauka*, like the German *Wissenschaft*, has a wider meaning than the English word 'science', being often applied to many studies that we prefer to classify among the 'humanities' – philological science, economic science, pedagogic science, and so forth. Nevertheless, the difference in emphasis remains. Facilities for scientific study at higher level are expanding faster than those for the 'arts' side, yet the run on them is increasing even faster. Competition for entry to arts faculties is keen; for most science faculties it is positively fierce.

The emphasis on science as a major part of general education is evident early in the school. Scientific subjects are introduced gradually, until by the eighth year they take up nearly forty per cent of the week's teaching time – very nearly half if one includes the technical subjects. (In the thirty-one-hour week in class VIII, there are six hours of mathematics, three of physics, two of chemistry, two of biology, and one of technical drawing. Work-training takes up two hours, optional subjects three, and the humanities, social studies, and physical education the rest of the time.) In the secondary stage of the ten-year course (classes IV to X), scientific subjects account for over thirty-eight per cent of the time, work-training some eight per cent (not counting external periods of practice), nearly twelve per cent for art, music, and physical education, and upwards of forty per cent for the humanities and the social studies. The school week has been lightened over the last few years, while the proportion of science and technology has increased.

The reasons for this are partly practical. Like any other major industrial country, the Soviet Union has a large and growing need for highly-trained scientists, theoretical and applied, of all kinds. The experience of the early years, when acute shortages of educated manpower and the urgency of the problems to be tackled made necessary conscious efforts to tap every possible source, including the use of 'crash' programmes, has had a lasting effect; this is one explanation of the Soviet authorities' acute awareness of the importance to the developing national economy of adequate facilities for the training of scientists. Past experience, too, of having to make do with seriously under-trained people must have pressed home the lesson that even the most generous provision for scientific higher education is seriously handicapped unless it is strongly based on the ordinary schools.

There is also an ideological basis for this. In the Marxist–Leninist view, stress on scientific education for the sake of the betterment of the economy is a praiseworthy aim, but limited. One of the main functions of the Soviet school, as we have seen, is to 'mould the materialist world outlook of the pupils'. Instilling Marxist views into the young involves, among other things, playing up the scientific attitude as the only way to the truth, and using it as a discouragement of any tendencies towards mystical or religious thinking. Marxist teaching is fundamentally 'rationalist' in its approach; it is only to be expected, therefore, that a Marxist state will emphasize the importance of the natural sciences in the upbringing of its young people.

Polytechnical Education

Linked with the scientific bias of Soviet education is the present policy of 'polytechnical education', one of the central points in the reforms of 1958 and after. Polytechnical education (*Politekhnicheskoe obrazovanie*) is defined by the Soviet authorities as an education based on the fundamentals of industrial production; it is quite distinct from trade training, which involves the acquisition of a particular vocational skill. Its aim is to make children familiar with the most important branches of production in industry and agriculture, imparting skills in the handling of tools and material, and generally acquainting them with both theoretical knowledge and first-hand practical experience of the

43

basic processes of production. Government policy requires that this combination of work theory and practice be combined with the more familiar school subjects to form the basic general education of the future Soviet citizen. Study and work alike must be familiar to him, whatever his future job may be. This, it is felt, makes for the fuller development of the child, since it broadens his horizons, improves his moral development (by getting him used to working with others – and for others), and makes for cohesion in Soviet society by ensuring a common experience of all sections of the people; the manual and the mental worker will feel less of a gulf between them when both have been taught how the other's job fits the needs of the community, and have had to learn something of the tasks and skills involved. This policy is also intended to benefit the national economy. The U.S.S.R. is still suffering from an acute manpower shortage as a result of the losses of the Second World War; the advantages of getting the schools to produce a better-trained labour-force, which could make some useful work-contribution while still learning, may well have weighed more heavily with the authorities than the purely ideological considerations.

It will be necessary to examine more fully the implications of polytechnization when we come to look at the present structure of the school system and the recent reforms that have made such sweeping changes in Soviet education. For the moment, it is worth remembering that there is nothing new about polytechnization; its recent reintroduction was made to serve a present need, but it has been in the air since the revolution and before. Karl Marx advocated the combination of academic study and productive labour (*Capital*, Book I, and elsewhere). Lenin, Krupskaya, and many others strongly supported the idea, but attempts to carry it into effect in the 1920s ended in complete failure, as did the use of 'progressive' educational methods, when excess of enthusiasm and doctrinaire application of the principle resulted in such a low standard of general education that the re-action of the 1930s went to extremes in the other direction, and the Soviet school settled into a long period of highly verbal, academic, formal instruction, from which it has only recently and partially emerged. Polytechnical education made a come-back in the decisions of the Nineteenth Congress of the Communist Party in 1952, but according to Khrushchov, speaking at the Twentieth Congress in 1956, the result was a great deal of talk and very little action. As this was the Congress where the famous 'secret speech' began the systematic demolition of Stalin as father-figure, the delegates doubtless took less notice of educational issues than they might have done in less disturbing circumstances. Nonetheless, polytechnization was extended, though the academic bias remained. In 1958, following Khrushchov's further advocacy of it, a greater degree of polytechnical education became one feature of the reform of the entire educational system. But there has been continual controversy on the form that it should take; in 1964, after frequent complaints about the repetitive nature of much of the labour training and production practice that went on, the time for these activities was reduced and the work rationalized, especially in the senior forms. In 1966, it was reduced still further, and the emphasis shifted back from factory and farm practice to work in school workshops and plots; only a third of the country's secondary schools – those near factories with adequate training facilities – continued with external production practice. It is still claimed, however, that the polytechnical principle is a central feature of the Soviet school. Some external work-practice has been reintroduced, with a particularly heavy involvement in the ninth class, and although the amount of time devoted to it is still less than it was at the high point of the 1958 law, both current practice and the Basic Law of 1973 confirm its continuing importance in the educational process.

Sex Equality

It has always been claimed that there is complete equality of the sexes in the Soviet Union, in education as in other fields. 'Women and men,' declares Article 35 of the Constitution, 'have equal rights in the U.S.S.R. Exercise of these rights is ensured by according women equal access with men to education and vocational and professional training, remuneration and promotion,

45

and in social, political and cultural activity.' It goes on to list supportive measures such as special labour regulations, paid maternity leave, and the gradual reduction of working time for mothers with young children. This, in contrast with the position before the revolution, was something of a novelty in the early days, especially in the areas of the Caucasus and Central Asia where Muslim tradition was strong.

But, as other countries have found, it is one thing to declare in favour of equality of opportunity in education for both sexes, and another to decide the best way of achieving it. It is universally recognized that boys and girls develop at different rates, have different emotional needs, and even in the U.S.S.R., where practically all women work whether they are married or not, have different educational needs where their future roles in the home are concerned. It is possible to argue that equality in education means the *same* education for both, and that differentiation always leads to some inequality. On the other hand, it can be urged that because of their differences equal treatment must involve *separate* education that will take account of the particular needs of both sexes. The final decision usually depends on whether the differences or similarities are thought to be more important.

Soviet policy has switched twice on this issue. Until 1943, co-education was the rule throughout the U.S.S.R. In the atmosphere of female emancipation after the revolution, segregation would have been regarded as reactionary and therefore unthinkable. In 1943 the situation was reviewed. Supported by discussion in the Press, a Decree was issued separating the sexes in the schools. In point of fact, the decision was never fully implemented. In the cities and bigger towns it was put into effect, but in the country it was difficult, in the remote areas impossible. In regions where many of the pupils lived far from the nearest school it was difficult enough as things stood to keep the schools running effectively without adding the further complication of separate but parallel schools for boys and girls. Except in the main population centres, therefore, co-education went on as before.

46

In 1954, public pulse-taking began again with the usual round of letters to the papers, meetings, and the like. Much of it may have been little more than window-dressing to justify decisions already taken – this was certainly the case on earlier occasions. Canvassing of senior officials behind the scenes probably still carried more weight than the public controversies. But, however the decision was reached, the result this time was the reintroduction of co-education throughout the school system, and those schools which had been segregated were speedily reorganized. This is the position at present. Apart from attending separate classes for physical education in the older forms, and some division of the sexes arising from the teaching of domestic science, boys and girls work together for everything – in the classrooms, workrooms, laboratories, and in the extra-curricular bodies such as the youth organization. Even the boarding schools are mixed, as a matter of policy as well as convenience. Co-education may still be a live issue in some other countries, but in the U.S.S.R. it appears to have come to stay and is confirmed as a basic feature of the system in the legislation currently in force.

Whether co-education and the whole battery of legal and other provisions ensure complete equality is less certain. That girls and women are entitled to equal treatment is beyond question; but it still needs to be asked how far they are able to take advantage of it. As so often happens, the general picture is one of substantial improvement, but there is still evidence to suggest that there is, in practice, still some way to go.

In the general school system, girls do rather well on the whole; they tend to predominate in the upper classes of the ten-year schools, to the extent that some minor social problems emerge, such as a shortage of boys at school dances. (The boys are rather more likely to be at schools with a technical bias from the age of fifteen, and are sometimes heard to complain about a shortage of girls at *their* dances.) In higher education, the picture is rather uneven, but by and large the position of women is favourable by most international standards. The proportion of women students has fluctuated over the years: it reached fifty-three per cent in the early 1950s, dropped to forty-three per cent a decade later, and has been rising again since then. In 1977, the figure had reached fifty-one per cent, and seemed to have stabilized. In the secondary specialized schools, which provide training for what might be loosely termed 'second-level' professions, the proportion of women is higher – fifty-five per cent on average.

Within higher education, there is considerable variation from one subject-group to another. Women dominate teacher training at the higher level (sixty-eight per cent) and even more at the secondary specialized level (eighty-three per cent), where kindergarten teachers (and, for the present, many primary teachers too) are trained. The huge preponderance of women in medical secondary specialized schools (eighty-nine per cent) is perhaps not surprising, as these are trainee nurses or auxiliaries; but at the higher level, where medical practitioners are trained, they are still in a clear majority (fifty-seven per cent), though less overwhelmingly than in the immediate post-war period. Medicine in the Soviet Union does not have the prestige or high income that it does in the U.S.A. or the U.K., but in engineering, which does enjoy high esteem and rewards in the U.S.S.R., women account for forty per cent of the student body. In spite of the survival of some of the traditional subject-orientation by sex, then, it would seem that women are well placed in higher education compared with most other countries. This is much less true of post-graduate study and academic employment; men students, for example, are twice as likely as women to go on to the first post-graduate degree. Sooner or later, apparently, a point is reached where sex proves to be some obstacle to opportunity and attainment, whatever the legal guarantees might be.

A similar pattern can be seen in the teaching profession. There, women are in the great majority (seventy-three per cent). There are variations in the different categories: men are in the majority in such subjects as labour training, music, art, and physical education, while seventy-nine per cent of other class teachers are women. But this is not reflected in the senior posts; eighty-three per cent of primary school heads are women, but there are very few separate primary schools. In the secondary schools, most heads are men; only at *assistant* director level are women in a majority. This pattern of diminishing equality the higher up one goes is found in other professions.[3]

Part of the problem is practical. The vast majority of Soviet women have jobs, but regularly complain that they have to work a 'second shift' (i.e. housework) as well. The difficulties of combining the roles of worker, housewife, and mother are familiar enough elsewhere, but in some ways are particularly acute in the U.S.S.R. Shopping, for instance, can be a slow and exhausting business, and having to rely (usually) on public transport means that it has to be done often; the growth of supermarkets and car ownership has a long way to go before this burden will be lightened appreciably. The survival of traditional attitudes does not help either; although most Soviet women do their bit by holding down full-time jobs, their menfolk are generally unwilling to do *their* bit by helping with the house and the children. According to a survey some years ago, in only a quarter of households did the husband give any help at all. These were mainly the younger husbands, which suggests that attitudes will change over time, but it is likely to be a slow process.[4]

There is evidence in employment also. Claims that lack of promotion is entirely due to one's sex are, of course, notoriously difficult to prove; but there have been complaints in plenty, and some cases have been so glaring that no other interpretation was possible. Some years ago, an investigation into a shortage of agricultural machine operators revealed that there were in fact plenty of trained people, but they were girls, and very few of them had managed to find jobs. Apparently there was too much hostility from the collective farm managements, who might put up with women doctoring them or teaching their children, but would not countenance their interfering in 'man's work'; a great many of the farm workers took the same view.

Even within the school system the law has been difficult to enforce, especially in former Muslim areas.[5] A recent investigation of the drop-out rate of girls from secondary schools in Azerbaidzhan found that some of them had left to get married under the legal age (one of them was only thirteen); the school director, unable to do much about it, had concealed this by keeping them on the register and even inventing regular marks for them. In extreme cases, the totally illegal practice of paying 'bride-price' still survives; in Turkmenia, it is said, the least well-educated girls command the highest prices, while the cheapest of all are those with higher educational qualifications, because 'they know too much and will not submit to their husbands as dutiful servants'. Such cases are not common, and cause major rows when brought to light; but that they can happen at all is an indication of the survival of attitudes that were officially abolished long ago; they also serve as a useful reminder of the limitations of political power.

Comprehensive Schooling

Soviet schools, except for a number of specialist schools which will be dealt with later, are completely comprehensive. Officially, every school of general education caters for the entire age-group, regardless of intelligence or attainment, of the area which it serves. Within each school, the comprehensive principle is carried to extremes; any kind of 'streaming' of the children into more and less able groups is forbidden. In this, the Soviet school goes farther than comprehensive schools in most other countries. The device of 'setting', extensively used in the U.K. comprehensive schools, whereby a child may be in a top section for, say, English and French but in a lower one for mathematics, is likewise excluded. Not only does the Soviet system reject the segregation of pupils into grammar-school-type and secondary-modern-type courses, but rejects any kind of segregation within the school. Every class is thus expected to have a complete cross-section of ability, from the brilliant to the plodder, all doing the same courses at the same pace. In the larger schools several classes are found in each year or grade, but are not divided by ability – children are allocated to these according to the streets they live in, the order their names come in the alphabet, or by some other non-scholastic standard.

This is a startling situation for many Western observers, still accustomed to the idea that different classes for different levels of ability are unavoidable, even though the schools themselves may be non-selective. Though the comprehensive school is much more familiar and acceptable than it was, even among many of a relatively traditional cast of mind, the practice of mixed-ability teaching is far less widely accepted by teachers or parents. In the U.S.S.R., *all* children are given the extensive course in the sciences mentioned before, all learn one foreign language, all go through the same course in history, geography, Russian, and so on. Difficulties arising from this are got round to some extent by encouraging the abler pupils to help those who are slower with their work – the 'arm round the book' mentality has no place here – and by putting so much emphasis on the virtues of hard work that some of the initially duller pupils can make up by sheer slog some of what they lack in native wit.

Among the results of this system are, on the credit side, some interesting performances in schools. It would be too much to expect that the entire age-group, or anything like it, could all reach the same fairly high official standard, but it does seem that there is some advantage in refusing to draw a firm line between the academically able minority and the rest, as happens in most Western European systems; more children make the grade than would be thought possible by those conditioned to the values of a selective system.

On the other hand, children who do not complete the work of the year satisfactorily have to take a further examination before the beginning of the next school year, and if they are still below standard they have to take that year again. During the 1960s the national average of 'repeaters' was around ten per cent, though lack of hard data makes it difficult to be sure about this. More recently, much has been made of attempts to get the numbers down, and of their general success; the figure now given is generally in the region of two per cent.[6] But some caution is called for. It is likely that standards can vary a good deal from school to school, and that if they were more strictly applied there would be rather more children repeating. Complaints have appeared in the Soviet Press about the tendency of some teachers to assess their pupils too leniently – an easy thing to do when so much use is made of oral examinations. Nevertheless, the schools do seem to bring a surprisingly high proportion of the population to a standard that we tend to think of as within the reach of the most able thirty per cent at best.

Apart from repeating, there are other ways in which the policy of the same course at the same pace for all can be modified. Children who are obviously mentally backward are educated along different lines in special schools run by the Ministry of Public Health, which is also responsible for the schools for the physically handicapped – those for cripples, epileptics, the deaf and the blind, the partially hearing and partially sighted, children with severe speech defects, and the like. Even there, however, the normal curriculum is followed as far as the seriousness of the defect permits; the aim of the special schools is not so much to compensate for a handicap as to correct it, and it is accepted as incorrigible only with the greatest of reluctance and after all attempts at remedy are thought to be exhausted. The concept of innate intelligence, though not entirely rejected by Soviet educators, is viewed with considerable distrust. Whenever possible, they seek a specific defect in a backward child rather than attribute his lack of progress simply to low intelligence.[7]

There are also unofficial ways of getting round the 'no streaming' problem. In spite of official insistence on uniformity of curricula and standards in schools of the same type, it often turns out that some schools are better than others, mainly due to the influence of the director and staff. Some schools with a lower standard tend to become dumping-grounds for children that other schools in the area can do nothing with; a good deal of passing pupils from school to school can take place, ending, sometimes, with the release of the least responsive children to blind-alley jobs before they reach the statutory leaving age. Such practices are totally unofficial and contrary to government policy, though the authorities must occasionally wink the eye for this to be possible at all. How much of this goes on is almost impossible to discover; the central authorities must be aware of it to some extent, but as we have seen they are often in no position to do much about it, especially in areas where the pressure of economic circumstances proves more powerful than regulations. But in all probability there are plenty of such malpractices that the central authorities themselves do not know about; local officials departing from the regulations are unlikely to advertise the fact if they can help it. The very existence of such practices is denied, of course, but from time to time references appear in the Soviet Press about, say, a gang of juvenile hooligans being brought up in court for some offence or other; it may come out that they were employed as general labourers at the Tallinn docks, and that they were mostly aged fourteen or even under, and therefore, officially, should not have been there at all, but at school. As often as not, such incidental disclosures lead to a row in the Press or in the teachers' journals, and some official is rapped over the knuckles or demoted. It is likely that if it were particularly common there would be more complaints and recriminations about it; however, the fact that such things can happen at all shows that the official position can be departed from in a number of ways even in a highly centralized system.

This rejection of streaming stems, fundamentally, from the Marxist insistence on the importance of environment in shaping a child's personality and abilities, rather than his hereditary equipment. Intelligence tests are condemned as 'bourgeois pseudo-science', at least as far as selection is concerned (they are conceded a limited role for diagnosis of the mentally handicapped); and although most will accept that levels of ability can differ, there is a great reluctance to consider 'intelligence' as something inborn and fixed. The Marxist believes that human nature is not basically pre-ordained, but rests in the hands of man himself; the Soviet educator accordingly regards the child as much more malleable than do most Western educators. He is likely to attribute failures not to his theories, but to misapplication of them or to practical difficulties like lack of space, inadequate pre-school training, or some such specific defect. Many Soviet teachers are less sure, having seen the differences in children's ability very clearly at first hand. They are liable to accept (up to a point and with caution) the idea of *some* degree of innate ability, and agree that these differences tend to raise problems in teaching unstreamed classes. But they will often argue that the social benefits of having all types of children working together more than compensate for the drawbacks of handling such mixed groups. The bright child may lose by not being able to forge ahead at his own pace; but the social training he receives in learning to help others instead of concentrating exclusively on his own advancement is felt to be one of the important foundations of communist morality. The emphasis is put on cooperation in the school rather than competition – which, if accepted, must certainly make unstreamed teaching easier than it would be here. But the difficulties persist. Even in the 1960s, attempts were being made to get round them by means of 'differentiated instruction', though many teachers were wary of the idea, lest it break up the class 'collective' and discourage slower pupils. Since then, however, the idea of some degree of differentiation (within a comprehensive framework) has gained strength, at official level as well as in the classroom. In 1965 the time for options in the senior classes was greatly increased (rising to six hours a week by the end of the course at that time), and the school or Pioneer clubs or 'study circles', which had provided extra opportunities for the more able child long before that, were extended. More recently, the principle of greater emphasis on individual or small group teaching has been accepted by the authorities, who now have the formidable task of training or re-training teachers for this more flexible but much more difficult approach.[8]

3. The Educational System:
General Characteristics (Part Two)

Discipline and Moral Education

In any kind of school, the most immediate aim in maintaining discipline is to make efficient teaching possible. There are some educationists who feel that they can teach in an atmosphere verging on permanent anarchy, but most teachers in most countries, and certainly in the U.S.S.R., are convinced that some degree of regulation is necessary to enable the teacher to get on with his job. But discipline, in the Soviet school and elsewhere, is regarded as more than a means of keeping the children in order while they are in the classroom – its aim is to have a more permanent effect in accustoming the child to certain ways of behaving and, if possible, thinking. In the Soviet scheme, discipline is essentially a means towards self-discipline; as well as making for the smooth running of classroom routine, it is intended to be part and parcel of the wider aim of moral education in shaping the future member of Soviet society.

For this reason, the familiar pattern of surrounding the child with a swarm of 'don'ts' is discouraged in the U.S.S.R. This is not to say that the detailed regulation of his conduct is disapproved of – on the contrary. But the stress is more on the positive side; exhortation rather than prohibition is the keynote, and the duties towards which he is exhorted are wide indeed.

Throughout the U.S.S.R., every child is expected to be familiar with, and observe, the twenty standard 'Rules for Pupils'[1] on which his disciplinary training is based. Not only are the children supposed to know *what* they are, but also *why* they are made, so that when a child is guilty of some misdemeanour the teacher may call on him to say which rule he has broken, and why he should have observed it. If the culprit is unable or unwilling to do this, another pupil will always oblige.

These rules are such a good guide to the comprehensive nature of Soviet discipline, and present such a clear picture of what the school requires of the children, that they are worth quoting in full:

It is the duty of every school child:

1. To acquire knowledge persistently in order to become an educated and cultured citizen and to be of the greatest possible service to his country.
2. To study diligently, to be punctual in attendance, and not arrive late for classes.
3. To obey the instructions of the school director and the teachers without question.
4. To arrive at school with all the necessary textbooks and writing materials; to have everything ready for the lesson before the teacher arrives.
5. To come to school clean, well groomed, and neatly dressed.
6. To keep his place in the classroom neat and tidy.
7. To enter the classroom and take his place immediately after the bell rings; to enter and leave the classroom during the lesson only with the teacher's permission.
8. To sit upright during the lesson, not leaning on the elbows or slouching; to listen attentively to the teacher's explanation and the other pupils' answers, and not to talk or let his attention wander to other things.
9. To rise when the teacher or director enters or leaves the room.
10. To stand to attention when answering the teacher; to sit down only with the teacher's permission; to raise his hand if he wishes to answer or ask a question.
11. To take accurate notes in his assignment book of homework scheduled for the next lesson, and to show these notes to his parents, and to do all homework unaided.
12. To be respectful to the school director and teachers; when meeting them, to greet them with a polite bow; boys should also raise their caps.
13. To be polite to his elders, to behave modestly and respectfully in school, in the street, and in public places.

14. Not to use coarse expressions, not to smoke, not to gamble for money or other objects.
15. To protect school property; to be careful of his personal things and the belongings of his comrades.
16. To be attentive and considerate of old people, small children, and the weak and the sick; to give them a seat on the bus or make way for them in the street, being helpful to them in every way.
17. To obey his parents; to help them take care of his small brothers and sisters.
18. To maintain order and cleanliness in rooms; to keep his clothes, shoes, and bed neat and tidy.
19. To carry his student's record book with him always, to guard it carefully, never handing it over to anyone else, and to present it on request of the teacher or school director.
20. To cherish the honour of his school and class and defend it as his own.

These rules go far beyond the needs of discipline in the narrower sense. Some of them, certainly, seem dictated by pure administrative convenience, others are concerned more with formal etiquette than with anything more fundamental; but the total impression is not that of a battery of convenient regulations and nothing more. The object of holding up a code of this kind is to set a standard of behaviour and attitudes. Though many of the precepts have only an indirect connection with moral issues in the strict sense, they serve to condition the children to conduct themselves in the socially approved manner, which is the cornerstone of communist moral teaching. They also, incidentally, serve to minimize the confusion that might result from the arbitrary variations of discipline that can be found from one class to the next in more loosely organized systems; the picture of society's expectations is constant throughout.

The Soviet school takes moral education very seriously indeed; no less seriously than instruction in, say, the basic skills or the sciences. The reason is not far to seek; we have seen that the overriding purpose of education is to serve the needs of Soviet society by preparing its future citizens according to requirements, and moral education is, in the Marxist view, an aspect of political education. There is little likelihood, therefore, of moral teaching being confined to the occasional pious platitude from the teacher in the course of ordinary lessons. Platitudes there are in plenty, but this is held to be totally insufficient. If Soviet education is to succeed in its basic purpose, children have to be taught what are considered to be the right values, and put in the frame of mind to act accordingly.

The Marxist view of ethics rules out any supernatural or metaphysical basis for moral values. Broadly, it regards a moral code as a device to serve the needs of the society in which it is current, an aid to securing the loyalty and cooperation of citizens, a stimulus to effort for the common good, or as a simple lubricant (in the form of politeness, consideration, etc.), which helps the wheels of society to run more smoothly. Communist morality is thus socially derived, and consequently has many features peculiar to the needs of Soviet society such as love for the Soviet Motherland, pride in the revolutionary traditions, loyalty to the precepts of Lenin, the Soviet government, and the Communist Party. Many of the other precepts are familiar in most societies, as when children are exhorted to be unselfish, kindly, hardworking, honest, and so forth. Some communist writers on morality argue that the basic virtues are self-evidently and absolutely good. This, of course, does not take the argument very far ('good is good because it is good', as it were), nor does the idea that *all* morality is based on class interest, which is demonstrably untrue. Many Marxists now state that certain basic moral values are valid for all societies, since they operate to the benefit of mankind at large. This does not mean that they feel the need of any divine or metaphysical standard – the basic values are derived from the needs of social man. The main difference is that whereas these virtues are presented in most other countries as absolutes in their own right, or as conduct pleasing to God, they are esteemed and encouraged in the Soviet school for their social utility in smoothing personal relations, and in making the child more ready to work selflessly for the wellbeing of the community, an essential attribute to the 'new man' whom the Soviet educators are striving to produce.

The aim of moral teaching, then, is to produce a person who

will be willing and able to put all the effort of which he is capable into work for the common good, building the new society under the guidance of the Communist Party and, furthermore, finding joy and fulfilment in the task. This is a more ambitious objective than merely getting people to behave themselves, which can sometimes be difficult enough. To have any hope of even partial success, it needs both careful planning and the mustering of all available resources; this, in large measure, is what the Soviet educational system does.

Moral education is a joint enterprise, in which the school, the youth organizations, parents' bodies, and others are all expected to play their parts. As far as the school is concerned, every effort is made to utilize any possible means of putting across the ideas and practice of communist morality, such as class organization, teacher's example, direct preaching, sloganizing, or anything else that can be brought to bear. Moral education is given a prominent place in teachers' training courses; the statement that 'it is important not just to produce teachers of subjects but teachers of children' comes to the lips of tutors in Pedagogic Institutes no less frequently than their Western counterparts, and is backed up with special textbooks and schemes of instruction on the subject. Problems of moral education are considered legitimate fields for study and research on a par with more conventional topics; the schemes of work in this field are just as detailed and carefully thought out. The Academy of Pedagogic Sciences worked out a graded scheme for moral education,[2] detailing the various character traits and behaviour patterns thought appropriate to children of different age levels, a scheme which forms the framework for much of the direct moral teaching in the schools.

Space does not permit a full acount of this scheme, but some examples will suffice to show the scope of the objectives the teacher is expected to try to attain. At the elementary level, roughly from the age of seven to eleven, the school is to inculcate a wide range of character traits calculated to lay the foundations of 'communist character' in the children. Though there is no suggestion that they can be tackled in logical sequence, they are grouped for convenience into eight principal categories:

1. Elementary ideas of good and bad.
2. Love of the Motherland.
3. Industriousness and frugality.
4. Truthfulness, honesty, modesty, and kindness.
5. Friendship and comradeship.
6. Discipline.
7. Love of studies and conscientiousness.
8. Good social conduct in the school, at home, in the streets, and in public places.

These categories are wide and comprehensive. For example, the second – Love of the Motherland – embraces the following: to respect the work of adults for the common good and the welfare of the family, and to bring adults joy through success in study and conduct; to love one's school, to develop the ability to study well, to respect the teacher; to love the native locality; to take an interest in the heroic past and present of the Motherland, to have a warm love for V. I. Lenin, to have a feeling of gratitude to the Communist Party and the Soviet government; to have a feeling of friendship for the children of all nations; to hate instigators of wars; to have the desire to be good Octobrists or Pioneers. The fact that all these traits are grouped under 'Love of the Motherland' shows how far basic Soviet morality is rooted in the needs of society as a whole, in the minds of the educators at least.

Again, 'Love of studies and conscientiousness', the seventh category, includes: to be curious, listen attentively, read, observe, work, study, and create; to carry out all requirements and teacher's instructions with a degree of independence; to apply the acquired knowledge of life and share it with others. The eighth category, 'Good social conduct in the school, at home, in the streets, and in public places', is even more detailed and all-embracing; the details of this are: to be orderly, neat, and well-groomed; to be polite, using the common forms of politeness such as 'Good morning', 'Please', 'Thank you', and so forth, and to look affable during conversation and not interrupt each other; to behave properly at home, leaving and entering the house quietly and without banging doors, and asking permission to take anything or leave the house; to conduct oneself properly in the streets and in public places, obeying the rules of conduct in cinemas, dining-rooms, libraries, etc., to be on time, to wipe footwear at the entrance, not to run about, not to break line, not to speak loudly; to prevent comrades from committing bad actions. Most of the categories of behaviour are thus analysed to indicate general principles and the details of everyday conduct. Such schemes go beyond the 'Rules for Pupils', which are a prop for wider moral teaching, as outlined above.

Methods are as precise and detailed as the aims. The teacher has a long list of activities in the school that can be used to put across the desired points. These are grouped under the following general headings: (1) Preparation for the school year, (2) First days in class, (3) Cooperation with the Pioneers, (4) Cooperation within the home, (5) Personal example of the teacher, (6) Common welfare, (7) Celebration of certain days, (8) Themes, story-telling, reading, dramas, (9) Preparation for the summer. In general, the teacher is expected to make deliberate use of practically any school experience or activity, in the classroom or out of it, to influence in the prescribed direction the child's behaviour and development of moral values. He is also expected to get through the scheme by the end of the fourth year, when the child is about eleven; by that time the elementary foundations of morality should have been established, so that the child can proceed to the next, and more elaborate, stage.

At this second stage, the child is now under the influence, not of one all-purpose class teacher, but of several subject specialists and a 'form teacher' whose job it is to ensure team coordination and have a special eye to the welfare and moral education of the particular class. At this level, the moral traits to be encouraged are in some cases the same as the earlier ones, with a change in emphasis from habit-forming to rational appreciation of the need for them, and their place in the whole structure of Soviet society. Here are a few of the items involved: (1) Soviet patriotism and a feeling of friendship among peoples. This includes, among other things, love of one's own locale, respect for historic revolutionary and other monuments, understanding of the superiority of the Soviet over the bourgeois system, working for the good of the native land, taking a lively interest in the activities of the Communist Party, the Soviet government, and the youth movement, taking an active part in the work of the Pioneers, taking an interest in the life and culture of peoples of other lands, and loving the children of workers the world over. (2) Realization of social duty. (3) Discipline, persistence, and endurance, including 'distinguishing between caution and cowardice, between boldness and recklessness'. (4) Friendship and comradeship, one instance of which is 'telling a comrade tactfully the truth to his face and helping him to find the right solution'. (5) Attentive and thoughtful attitudes towards people. (6) Truthfulness, honesty, and modesty; apart from the avoidance of lying, this taken to comprise having a 'proper attitude' to criticism, being able to resist bad influences such as 'rowdyism, profanity, gambling, drinking, idleness, excessive fondness of motion pictures and football', avoidance of boasting about the position of one's parents, or of attracting attention by 'loud clothing or accentuated manners'. (7) Responsible attitudes towards study and work; apart from the expected exhortations to diligence, we find included here the application of knowledge and skills to life for the common welfare, and the showing of concern for the study achievements of the whole class.

The methods used for putting over such virtues to the children are much the same as in the earlier classes, but with more conscious participation on the part of the pupils, who join in the discussions about the programme of activities for teaching the scheme. This serves not only to make the teaching more immediate, but makes the commitment of the older ones to the values expressed more definite, since activity is always more effective than mere preaching. Most of the work on the staff side inevitably falls on the 'form teacher', but subject specialists are expected to relate their own work to the programme as well, while the parents and the Pioneers, by giving support to the teacher and reinforcing what is taught in the classroom, help to complete the process. Habits of performing 'socially useful labour' – voluntary work for the community, organized by the school and the Pioneer organization – are thought to be especially valuable, since this accustoms the children to work for others, and shows them how their efforts can do good in some specific, tangible way that they can understand. There are many activities of this kind, including such work as collecting scrap metal for factories, weeding communal gardens, helping crippled war veterans with their housework, even more elaborate tasks such as helping to lay out a playground for pre-school children in the neighbourhood, or building radio sets for invalids. Some of these tasks are officially organized, but many *appear* to arise spontaneously from the children themselves, which is considered particularly praiseworthy, and is reported frequently and prominently in *Pionerskaya Pravda* and other children's periodicals. The frequency with which this happens *seems* to show that the aims of the school in moral education have a considerable degree of success. Words are always cheap, but action suggests a much more real conviction – if the description is to be trusted.

In the senior classes the emphasis in moral training is more towards personal and social responsibility, and is aimed more specifically at the fitting of young people for their duties as adults, members of families, workers, and citizens of the U.S.S.R. Many of the moral precepts dealt with in the earlier years still feature in the scheme, but the stress is now more on political attitudes, correct understanding of social theory, and personal responsibility to the 'collective' or group, whether national, local, or personal. Loyalty to the precepts of Marx and Lenin, to the policy of the Communist Party, the Komsomol, the Soviet government and people, and the Motherland, figure prominently, as might be expected. Stressed also are the obligations to action of all kinds – in work, study, 'agitation' (explaining and defending Party policies), in studying to raise one's 'theoretical and ideological level', and in combating local nationalism and racialism as well as 'loafers, slackers, thieves, and those who would damage public property'. In the field of personal values and conduct, pupils must be taught to be modest in relation to other people, to maintain friendly relations between the sexes (presumably this means that youths must treat girls as equals, not just as potential sexual partners), to be intolerant of all forms of humiliation and insults to other people, to be intolerant of 'abnormal and amoral acts, and all indications of disrespect, boasting, haughtiness, and other violations of the norms of socialist humanism', not to violate Soviet laws and to keep others from violating them, to aid those in need, to be intolerant of 'uncomradely attitudes' towards women, and so forth. These are only a few of the character traits that the authorities see as essential ingredients of what they call 'moral Soviet man'.

As before, the methods used to inculcate the desired attitudes and conduct range over all fields of school and extra-curricular work. Debates, discussions, lectures, and the like are brought in to ensure understanding of the moral code, while 'socially useful labour', political work in the youth organization, and routine school studies, are intended to reinforce these desirable attitudes by turning them into habitual actions.

The attention paid to moral education in the Soviet school, then, is considerable, and appears to be effective on the whole, though of course it does not produce the generation of selfless paragons visualized by schemes such as the one outlined above. This effectiveness is due to some extent to the general atmosphere in Soviet society, conducive to conformity and collective action at all levels. But this is not enough; it might cow pupils into dull acquiescence, but little more. There are some young people who kick over the traces and go in for some kind of delinquency, possibly as a protest, but for the most part the impression of urban Soviet schoolchildren is one of earnest, even naïve, concern for their own prowess and their duty to the 'collective', which seems based on sincerity rather than any need to go through the motions. Social conformity doubtless has much to do with it; so has the continual barrage of politico-moral sloganizing to which the child has been subjected, in school and out, from his earliest years. But it would be a mistake to exaggerate the importance of this aspect; the success of moral teaching in the schools is mainly due to the care with which it is planned and presented, to the determination, so typical of Soviet education, to leave nothing to chance. Significantly, every aspiring teacher, specialist or not, must take a course in the theory of moral education as part of his basic curriculum.

With such ambitious aims in moral education and discipline, more immediate problems might seem relatively unimportant. This is true in a sense; order is the means to the end, not the end itself. But it is recognized that it is no less important for all that – as we have seen, it is one of the main props for the wider aims, as well as an obvious necessity if any work is to be done. A great deal of attention is therefore paid to problems of dealing with the lazy, stubborn, or rebellious child.

Soviet teachers are discouraged from relying too much on fear of punishment. They are urged rather to use positive methods, such as pointing out the ill-effects of the child's wrongdoing. Nevertheless, they do have at their disposal a carefully graded system of punishments for use when necessary. Corporal punishment is not one of these; violence to children is condemned by theory, disapproved of by public opinion, and forbidden by law. (In this, the Soviet Union is of the same mind as most other countries, with the exception of Britain and one or two others.) But there are other measures available, ranging from a reproof from the teacher to expulsion from the school. Reproofs and reprimands are of varying degrees of severity; they may come from the class teacher or the director of the school, they may be private or public, they may be mild in tone and content or heavy with menace for the future if better behaviour is not forthcoming. Like all punishments, they are supposed to be noted in the pupil's record, which details his school work and conduct from the day he enters the school to the end of his course. In the vast majority of cases, a moderate reprimand seems to be enough. If not, the teacher may keep the child in after school for extra work; he may have the child suspended from the Pioneer organization, which is felt to be a great disgrace, as the child thus deprived of the right to wear his red scarf feels conspicuous as long as his suspension lasts – usually about a term. The teacher may even take the step of lowering the pupil's conduct mark, a very serious matter indeed. All school subjects are marked on a five-point scale, from one (very bad) to five (excellent). A complete record of these marks is kept to show the child's day-to-day progress. In ordinary subjects a four or even a three is quite passable, but for *conduct* nothing less than a five will do. If the conduct mark is reduced to four, the pupil is in effect under threat of expulsion, for if there is no sign of improvement within a short time it can then be reduced to three, the signal for his ejection from the school. Since the pupils (and their parents) know this from the start of their school careers, things seldom go as far as this.

It is seldom, in fact, that the teacher has to use more than a small part of his battery of punishments, for the children frequently take a hand themselves. If one of their number is behaving badly, or is lazy at his work, they tend to take this as letting them and the school down, having been conditioned from their earliest days to the idea of the social duty of work and collective responsibility. Before official action has gone beyond a reprimand or two, therefore, the defaulter is likely to find himself at a meeting of his classmates in the school Pioneer room, where they solemnly discuss his shortcomings, point out the error of his ways, appeal to him to remember his duty to the class, the school, the Motherland, the building of communism. If the trouble stems from his inability to cope with the classwork, they will offer to coach him during free time. If the child is still obdurate, or refuses to attend the meetings at all, they will discuss his case carefully and deliberate what to do. They may decide to 'send him to Coventry', or make fun of him in the class wall-newspaper, if they feel that cold-shouldering or ridicule are likely to have any effect. Usually, they do – few children like to find suddenly that nobody will speak to them, or can shrug off caricatures of themselves as free-wheeling passengers on a multiple bicycle which everyone else is furiously pedalling uphill 'on to the building of communism', or seeing themselves pilloried as 'traitors to the future of the Soviet Union', if their classmates are taking an unusually stern line. It can be seen why teachers rarely have to unleash their full powers on badly behaved children, for only the hardened or the completely indifferent are likely to withstand such pressures from their classmates. Even with real 'problem children', group pressure can do much; in such cases the cruder methods of ostracism and satire are less likely to be used, as they do more harm than good, but the children will try to win the difficult ones over by drawing them into their games and activities if they can. In short, class opinion is on the teacher's side and is quick to organize for action, a situation which makes the teacher's job of keeping order infinitely easier than where it is taken for granted (as in some schools here) that it must always be a battle between teacher and class.

There are other means of securing class order as well as those mentioned. As we shall see presently, steps are taken to ensure that the school has the support of the parents, which helps enormously. Besides this, and the continual pressure on the child to work hard and behave well as a moral and social duty, self-interest plays its part too. For the vast majority of children (more than ever if the current onslaught on nepotism and string-pulling proves effective) the only way to personal advancement is through education. For any youngster at all ambitious, a good school record is absolutely essential. Most children realize this, and behave accordingly. There are a few who are stubborn, mal-adjusted, or lazy, to an extent that defies all treatment; there are a few who resent the continual pressures and are strong-minded enough to show it and put up with the consequences. These are the casualties of an educational system that makes heavy demands on its pupils, some of whom develop into Soviet delinquents, the *stilyagi* and *guligany*. But the great majority do behave and do work hard; in this way they can conveniently yield to overwhelming social pressure, reap personal advantage, and perform their moral and patriotic duty at one and the same time.

Family and School

Even the most far-reaching school systems have the children in their charge only part of the time. During a child's school career, therefore, the school is only one of the influences on his character and development, however carefully planned its work may be. Further, compulsory schooling in the U.S.S.R. does not begin until the child has reached the age of seven, by which time his personality and inclinations have already been shaped to a considerable degree. The effectiveness of what the school teaches, therefore, depends largely on its ability to ensure cooperation outside. Of these other influences, the most important is the family; this is the first group with which the child comes in contact, and it provides the environment in which most of his time is spent during his formative years. Appreciating this, Soviet educators take great care to make sure that the family is on their side. Passive approval, as in other things, is not enough; the school uses every available means to enlist the parents as active supporters of its work, and to make them conscious of the family's role as 'the primary cell of socialist society'.

There are many ways of doing this, the most effective being the association of parents with the active running of the school. Every class has its parents' meeting. This is convened by the director of the school at the beginning of the session, and meets in the appropriate form-room with the teacher as chairman. Some of the time may be spent looking at exhibitions of classwork, listening to the teacher lecturing on some aspect of the children's education, or congratulating each other (as is the custom) on the beginning of the new school year. The parents of the class will meet as a group once or twice every term to discuss general problems or to hammer out particular difficulties; the principal purpose of these meetings is to acquaint the parents with the work of the school in general and their own children in particular. At the first of these meetings, the parents elect three of their number (sometimes called the 'Parents' Trinity') to serve on the Parents' Committee of the whole school.

The school Parents' Committee is a more elaborate and formal organization, operating according to instructions from the Ministry of Education on composition, activities, and procedure. It elects a praesidium of eight members or more, including one from each year; this praesidium in turn elects a chairman, who is co-opted to the Pedagogic Council, which consists of the entire teaching staff of the school under the chairmanship of the director. The praesidium meets at frequent intervals (usually about once a fortnight) to deal with a variety of problems such as arranging help for parents who are having difficulty with their children, ensuring that the 'Rules for Pupils' are known and understood by all parents, and dealing with difficult cases by interviewing troublesome children, or their parents, or both. The Parents' Committee, through its praesidium, is also involved in discussion on the parents' role in the scheme for moral education; as with other school work, it sees that the aims are known to the parents and supplies advice (in consultation with the teachers) on practical ways in which they can help. The Committee also co-operates in the running of extra-curricular activities in the school, helping to supply leaders, instructors, material, equipment, and so forth. Generally, the function of the praesidium is to provide a permanent link between the whole body of the parents and the teachers. It ensures that both sides are aware of each other's problems, and is thus a means whereby parents can make their views (or worries) known to the staff. For the most part, however, it is concerned with seeing that parents are aware of their educational duties, and providing the knowledge and help necessary for carrying them out.

The Parents' Committee also organizes full-scale parents' meetings, and runs permanent sub-committees to deal with specific problems. The full parents' meetings take place about once a term, and are devoted partly to lectures by teachers to the whole group, and partly to meetings in the separate classrooms where the teachers give reports on the work of the class and the progress (or lack of it) of each pupil. The discussion that arises from this is often quite lively, and may go into some detail.

Among the permanent sub-committees found in any school are those on 'Training and Upbringing', which concern themselves with scholastic progress and discipline; 'Pedagogical Propaganda', which organize meetings, lectures, and generally deal with the spread of educational knowledge among parents; 'Cultural Mass Work', which help to run the extra-curricular activities such as 'circles', concerts, theatre visits, and excursions of all kinds; 'Sanitation', for the supervision of the school's dining-rooms, lavatories and washing facilities, and the like. The setting-up of these sub-committees is required by ministry regulation, though others may be appointed if necessary, at the discretion of individual Parents' Committees. There is no formal parents' organization above the level of the school.

Home and school contacts are not confined to committee work and formal meetings. The school director may call parents to the school for consultation, either singly or in groups; 'Parents' Trinities' can sit in on lessons to see them in action for themselves. As for the teacher, home visiting is regarded as part of his normal duties. This starts in the earliest classes and continues right up to the end of the school course. The object is partly to enable the teacher to get some idea of the child's home conditions, which can be useful in many ways – it might make all the difference to the tactics used in the case of disciplinary trouble, for example. Further, it gives the parents a chance to talk to the teacher in more familiar, and therefore more reassuring, surroundings, for some parents still find the school rather a daunting place.

Apart from such links between individual schools and parents, steps are taken to reach parents on a national scale. There are radio programmes dealing with a variety of educational topics, designed specially for parents. Many books and pamphlets are also issued, mostly couched in a simple, semi-fictional form, and the magazine *Semya i shkola* (Family and School), issued once a month, acts as a vehicle for information and, in the correspondence columns, a platform where parents can seek instruction or voice complaints. It is popular in tone and much brighter in style (though this is not saying a great deal) than most Soviet publications. Its circulation, which stood at about fifty thousand just after the war, has climbed to near the half-million mark in recent years.

It would be too much to expect this picture of close concord between the family and the school to be universally unblemished. Among difficulties met are the extremes (tryingly familiar to most British teachers) of the uncooperative parent on the one hand and the over-anxious parent on the other. The first is not, apparently, very common, but there are some parents who dismiss the whole system as unwarranted interference or, more usually, just drag their feet and do nothing. But the system is now so well established that they have the rest of the parents against them; if this pressure is insufficient, it is possible for the parents' trade union or factory committee to take an interest, which is harder to resist than the disapproval of neighbours. A recent case in Kiev can serve as an example; in the Krasny factory, a notice was pinned up (by another parent) to the effect that Anatoly Orlenko, Class IV pupil, was behaving badly at school. Orlenko senior speedily found himself before the factory committee, and was told that he ought to do something about this, since it reflected on the factory as well as the child, the parent, and the school. They pointed out that if Orlenko was unable to do anything because he lacked the knowledge, his best course would be to consult the appropriate organ of the Parents' Committee, or the teacher, who would certainly be able to help him with advice. It is not recorded what the father said, but most probably he was squirming with embarrassment by this time and was only too glad to comply, in case the committee brought the matter up at an open meeting and shamed him publicly before all his workmates. Techniques of this kind are effective, but rarely used; they are regarded as a drastic step to be used only when gentler methods have failed. Given the prevailing atmosphere among parents in the first place, it is hardly surprising that such bulldozing methods are exceptional.

Parents' concern for their children's future is at least one reason for the cooperation they give to the school, but it is from excess of such concern that other difficulties arise. Some parents, it seems, regard the school as a device for ensuring their *own* offspring's smooth passage into higher education and a 'white-collar' job, whatever may happen to anyone else. This can lead to the teacher's being badgered by the progress-hungry parent, who blames the teacher if the desired results are not forth-coming. (A similar situation is not unfamiliar here, as many teachers know to their cost.) Other parents, of the same turn of mind, look askance at work-training and 'socially useful labour', feeling that any form of manual work (*chornaya rabota*, 'black work', as they call it) is beneath their children's dignity. Worse still, if the parent happens to have an influence, particularly political influence, he may bring sometimes intolerable pressure to bear on the teacher to force his child's progress, or even to invent it. Such parents, when they have influence, can be a menace; even when they have not, they can be a thorough nuisance, and make cooperation between family and school difficult in the extreme – as it must always be when the two sides have different interests.

Pushing parents are probably commoner than stubborn ones, but both appear to be in a minority, and all the social pressures at the present time are likely to make these minorities still smaller. Most things are everyone's business in the Soviet Union, which makes the weight of opinion keenly felt by the deviant. The standing of the teacher helps too; the traditional Russian veneration for 'culture' and the Soviet régime's continual emphasis on the social importance of education combine to give the teacher some degree of social prestige. This makes the average Soviet parent ready to defer to his judgement, and offer help when asked for it. Thus, every point of contact between home and school is in theory maintained, parents are brought into the running of the school whenever feasible, relations between parents and teachers are cordial and respectful, and there can be little doubt that this makes the running of the school much easier and more effective. In this sense it is a partnership, both sides making their contribution to the child's upbringing. But the teachers are regarded as the senior partners, the experts. The school is firmly in control.

The Youth Movement

The work of the Soviet school is so closely linked with the youth organizations that they can be fairly described as an integral part of the educational system. From one point of view they are political organizations, and are thus part of the system insofar as its aims are the inculcation of communist doctrine; some of their functions are recreational, embracing the role played in Western countries by such bodies as the Boy Scouts, Girl Guides, Boys'

Brigade, church clubs, and youth clubs. But they also play a prominent part in the normal work of the school, in matters like helping with discipline, moral education, the tutoring of backward pupils, the provision of spare-time voluntary classes, and so forth. Significantly, the large amounts of money paid to the youth organizations by the State are reckoned in the budget under normal educational expenditure. The youth movement is voluntary, includes both boys and girls, and is organized in three stages: the Octobrists, for the younger children; the Pioneers, for children between the ages of ten and fifteen; and the Komsomol, for young people between fifteen and twenty-seven.

The Octobrists

Unlike the two senior branches, this is not a formal organization, but a rather vague preparatory stage for entry into the Pioneers. Any young pupil who behaves and does his work reasonably well can become a member, but there is no pressure to join, nor is the threat of expulsion used as a means of obtaining discipline – that comes later. Teachers often use informal Octobrist groups to organize children for any task requiring cooperation, such as tidying the classroom. As they approach the age of ten, however, their teacher, together with Pioneers from higher classes, teaches them about the Pioneer organization and its importance, the duties and privileges of membership, and acquaints them in advance with the Promise and Rules that they will be expected to know, much in the manner of a Cub-mistress preparing her charges for the 'going-up' ceremony into the Scouts.

The Pioneers

'I, a Young Pioneer of the Soviet Union, in the presence of my comrades solemnly promise to love my Soviet Motherland passionately, and to live, learn, and struggle as the great Lenin bade us and as the Communist Party teaches us.' Reciting this promise along with his fellows, the ten-year-old is admitted to the Pioneer Organization and receives from the Pioneer leader his triangular red scarf and the badge bearing the motto '*Vsegda gotov'*, 'Always ready'. Speeches made by the leader, and the ritual of the occasion impress on the child's mind the importance and responsibility of membership. At ceremonies of this kind, held in schools, in Pioneer Palaces, or in factories over the whole of the U.S.S.R., the great majority of schoolchildren formally enter the organization which will have more direct impact on their lives than any other while they are at school.

Although membership of the Pioneers is voluntary – in theory, a privilege – most children do in fact join as soon as they are eligible. A few individualists stay out, but they are rare; non-members are much more likely to have been suspended or even expelled from the organization for bad behaviour of some kind. This near-unanimity seems to be due mainly to the natural gregariousness of children – they all want to 'belong' – and to the fact that membership is treated as an honour from the time the child enters the school. A further incentive is the range of interests and activities that membership offers the child.

Strictly speaking, it is not necessary to join the movement to take part in the recreational activities it organizes. It is not an exclusive body like the Communist Party, but it is described officially as a 'mass organization'[3] for children. Accordingly, non-members are not only allowed but encouraged to take part in its activities, in the expectation (nearly always justified) that they will want to become members.

The range of activities is almost unlimited. Education for leisure is taken seriously by the Soviet authorities, and provided for by an extensive network of school clubs and out-of-school institutions, in which the Pioneer movement plays a leading part.[4] It provides or helps with clubs and 'circles' in the schools and elsewhere, in a variety of hobbies, arts, and crafts; these range from small painting or singing groups in an ordinary school to full-scale youth orchestras and ballet and drama groups in the Pioneer Palaces. Exhibitions, festivals, and competitions (known as 'Olympiads') are held frequently at local, republic, and Union level. This compensates to a great extent for the rather meagre treatment of the arts in the ordinary school curriculum. Many of the organization's centres have theatres where children can

74

produce and act their own plays, and there are also over a hundred theatres, puppet and live, which present plays specially for children.

In sport the position is much the same, though rather more attention is paid to it in the school curriculum as well. Games taught in the schools can be pursued in clubs and at Pioneer centres, as can many additional sports, from football and hockey to tennis and fencing. There is the usual variety of festivals and competitions, described, rather surprisingly, as 'Spartakiads' – the term 'Olympiad' is used for contests in the arts, school subjects, chess, and the like. There are also over a thousand Children's Sports Schools, where pupils can go during the holidays or in their spare time for practice and instruction. Millions of children every summer attend Pioneer holiday camps in the Caucasus, on the Black Sea coast, or similar places. There, as might be expected, sporting activities figure prominently.

The youth organizations do a good deal to encourage interest in nature and provide opportunities for its study. The Pioneers organize festivals, meetings, and excursions of all kinds. There are naturalists' circles in many schools and 'Young Naturalists' Stations' in different parts of the country. Their main emphasis is on fostering interest in agriculture, but they also encourage nature conservation, and have wild-life sections for activities such as bird-watching or entomology. Similarly, Children's Excursion-Tourist Stations combine sightseeing trips with the study of geography and natural resources. Children's Technical Stations run clubs for the pursuit of all kinds of skills from radio engineering to model-making, and Children's Railways afford entertainment as well as training in technical skills and organizational responsibility.

But the most important of all out-of-school institutions for children are the 2,600 Pioneer Palaces and Houses, where they can go in their free time to follow their hobbies and interests. Some of these centres, especially in the more remote country areas, are modest or even ramshackle, with limited space, scanty equipment, and a shortage of trained leaders. Others, like the Anichkov Palace in Leningrad or the Vorontsov Palace in Odessa, are former residences of the old aristocracy converted to a new use. Others again are modern and often sumptuous.

In this last category, the largest is the 'Pioneer Republic' in Moscow, opened in June 1962 and considerably extended since then. It is untypical in many ways: not only is it the newest building of the kind, but it is one of the few designed in uncompromisingly 'contemporary' style. There are few centres even approaching the variety of its facilities; but even if it cannot be taken as a typical example of Pioneer Palaces, it shows what the Pioneer Organization can, at its most generous, provide.

The building of the Pioneer Republic stands in the Lenin Hills (near Moscow University) in spacious grounds which take in, among other things, a sports stadium with a seating capacity of seven thousand, and an artificial lake where the children can build and sail boats. Inside, the entrance hall comprises a glass-domed winter botanical garden and a pool; there is a 'Hall dedicated to Lenin' and a 'Hall of International Friendship of Children', which house pictures, murals, statues, exhibitions, and models appropriate to their titles. There are buffets, canteens, and an amusement hall for young children, with swings and roundabouts in the shape of aeroplanes, helicopters, and the now inevitable space-ships. There are two theatres: one, where the children perform plays they have written, set, costumed, and produced (with the aid of one adult supervisor), seats over three hundred, is acoustically excellent, and has all the latest equipment in the way of lighting-boards, wing-space, dressing-room accommodation, and so forth; the other, where adult professionals perform, is somewhat larger. Other facilities include: lecture-rooms and laboratories for ordinary schools subjects, gymnasia, ballet- and dancing-rooms, art- and music-rooms, a planetarium, aeromodelling workshops, radio workshops, a photographic studio with dark-rooms, and a film studio with all normal equipment and ancillary premises. Altogether, this newest of Moscow's twenty-five Pioneer Palaces provides for sixty 'circles' and eight hundred groups; a child can join any two of these, which meet for seventy minutes twice a week, but no more, in case school work suffers. One wing yet remains to be built: this is to be designed

by the Young Architects' Circle (presumably with adult supervision and control) over the next year or so.

This gives some idea of the scope of the recreational side of
Pioneer activity at its maximum. But the All-Union Lenin
Pioneer Organization, to give it its full title, does not regard
recreational provision as its only, or even its major aim. Primarily
its functions are educational (political, moral, and social), as the
Pioneer Rules, a code of conduct rather than a set of regulations,
clearly show:

1. A Pioneer loves his Motherland and the Communist Party of the
   Soviet Union.
2. A Pioneer prepares himself to enter the Komsomol organization.
3. A Pioneer honours the memory of those who gave their lives in
   the struggle for freedom and for the prosperity of the Soviet
   Motherland.
4. A Pioneer is friendly to the children of all countries.
5. A Pioneer learns well.
6. A Pioneer is polite and well disciplined.
7. A Pioneer loves labour and is careful of public property.
8. A Pioneer is a good comrade: he cares for the young and helps the
   old.
9. A Pioneer is brave and unafraid of difficulties.
10. A Pioneer is honourable and values the honour of his detachment.
11. A Pioneer hardens himself, does physical exercises every day,
    and loves nature.

These rules are really a summary statement of the aims of
moral education described earlier, for the Pioneer Organization is
one of the principal means by which the educational system seeks
to translate its aims into reality. Class opinion is mobilized mainly
through the class Pioneer detachment, with ejection from its
ranks, a keenly felt disgrace, as one of its sanctions against
offenders. The 'socially useful labour', regarded as so valuable in
the inculcation of moral values, is organized by Pioneer groups.
The responsibility of the individual member to be an example to
other children is continually stressed, in school and out. In short,
from maintaining class order to the dissemination of social
attitudes, from the organizing of school societies to the coaching

of backward pupils, the Pioneer Organization is a constant and extremely effective ally of the teacher.

The structure of the Organization as well as its function is closely bound up with the school. The basic unit is the detachment (*otryad*), one for each class, further subdivided into 'links' (*zvena*) or small informal groups. The school as a whole has its brigade (*druzhina*).[5] All the Pioneers of the school elect a Brigade Council which coordinates most of the activities, guided by an adult Senior Pioneer Leader. The leader may be a professional, specially trained for this kind of work, but as these are in short supply[6] a member of the teaching staff often has to take over; Pioneer work is an essential part of every teacher's training course. Help is also given by Komsomols from outside the school, by student teachers, and in the case of schools with senior forms, by some of the older pupils.

The Komsomol

The all-Union Leninist Communist League of Youth (*Vsesoyuznyi Leninskii Kommunisticheskii Soyuz Molodyozhi*,[7] known as the VLSKM or Komsomol for short), is less directly linked with the school than its junior counterpart. The age range – fifteen to twenty-seven – is significant; membership thus includes senior pupils, students in higher education,[8] members of the armed forces, and workers in industry and agriculture. It is essentially an adult organization, designed to link the top end of school life with the first years of normal work. Much of the membership is adolescent, yet the tone of the organization is studiously adult throughout; there are no symbolic ceremonies on entry, there is no trace of uniform (except for the 'Red Flag' badge), and the stress in its activities is much more on political work and theory than it is in the Pioneers.

The Komsomol, like the Pioneers, is a 'mass' organization, but the mass is smaller. Although it does not screen applicants as carefully as the Communist Party, it is not as open-armed as the Pioneers with their almost complete membership. Of all young people eligible to go into the Komsomol, only about a third do so. This is partly from choice: membership can involve sometimes arduous duties, which many young people prefer not to assume; it can also involve loss of privacy, since members are expected to be an example to others, and are liable to be taken to task by their comrades if their conduct does not come up to exemplary standard.[9] But many of those who apply do so in vain; candidates have to prove their worth, not only politically but in study, work, and behaviour as well, and in spite of the falling-off in applications the Komsomol can still afford to pick and choose.

In structure, the Komsomol is closely modelled on the Communist Party. The basic unit, as in the Party, is the branch, always situated in the members' place of work – schools, universities, factories, farms, army units, and so on. Branches can be of any number from three to a hundred members, and are headed by branch secretaries. In the higher reaches, there are committees for each district (each with its bureau and secretary), for each region or city, and for each republic. The highest level is the Congress, which elects a central committee to continue with the work of the organization between the rather infrequent meetings of the full Congress. Branch secretaries are part-time and unpaid, but district secretaries and above are full-time professionals.

Admission to the Komsomol requires sponsorship, usually by the Council of the applicant's Pioneer Brigade; candidates not so sponsored need the recommendation of two established Komsomols or one established member of the Communist Party. Instead of the formal set of rules obtaining in the Pioneers, the Komsomol has a Charter listing a large number of members' rights and duties.[10] Rights include those of election to the various organs of the Komsomol, a vote in such elections, criticism of all persons and organs of the Komsomol, attendance when discussed by fellow-members, and so forth. Among the duties listed are the following: to improve one's knowledge of technology, to help implement Party policies and to explain them to others, to develop criticism and self-criticism, to set a good example in labour discipline, to take care of public property, to study Marxism–Leninism attentively, to be active in the Komsomol organization, and many others similar in content. Needless to say, not all members are as active as the Charter demands; in spite of constant attacks on 'passengers', and their occasional ejection from the organization, many remain. For the most part, however, the Komsomol's role as an 'agitation centre' for the spreading of acceptable attitudes among young people is maintained.

The work of the Komsomol is so widespread and diverse, extending into all fields of national life, that it would be inappropriate to try to examine it all here. The more strictly educational activities are channelled through its Congress, its publishing house, and the branches in schools and institutes of higher education.

The Congress of the Komsomol can serve as a forum for the discussion of general educational issues, thus forming a frame of reference in which the practical work at ground level can be done. The recent reforms of the educational system, for example, were first mooted at the Komsomol Congress. 'Bringing the schools closer to life' became a major topic of discussion right down the line. It is possible that some of the suggestions arising from such discussions had an effect on the final form of the law; and it is likely that having had it aired through the youth movement made it easier to put into effect.

At this level, too, the Komsomol exercises considerable control over the junior branches of the youth movement. It was the Central Committee in 1957 that raised the age for entry into the Pioneers to ten, and resurrected the Octobrists to fill the gap. The following year the Committee decided that there were too many Pioneers who were passive members and nothing more, and instituted a series of tests or 'steps', not unlike the Tenderfoot, Second Class, and First Class grades of the Scouts.[11] These steps involve the mastery of certain individual and collective skills, becoming more difficult with each step. Completion of the third grade will be expected of those applying for Komsomol membership.

The Komsomol organization also runs its own publishing house, *Molodaya Gvardiya*, or 'Young Guard'. As well as a variety of books for children and youths, it produces for the Pioneers the monthly magazine *Pioner*, and a twice-weekly newspaper, *Pionerskaya Pravda* (*Pioneers' Truth*), dealing with youth interests and activities all over the country, and the equivalent publications for the senior organization, the monthly *Molodoy Kommunist (Young Communist)* and *Komsomolskaya Pravda*.

School branches take a considerable share of the running of their schools. They elect committees to help with clubs and societies, they run debates and meetings, they discuss problems of discipline, moral education, and scholastic progress with the director, and act as Pioneer leaders to help the younger children with their part in the various tasks. They also make the teacher's job easier by keeping their own members and classmates in control; since the Komsomol is harder to get into than the Pioneers, membership carries more social prestige. Expulsion is accordingly more disgraceful, and its threat even more effective.

In the universities and other institutes of higher education, the Komsomol plays an important role too. Each faculty has at least one branch; there is a committee for the whole institute, whose representatives sit on every administrative body in the college, such as the committee for the allocation of hostel accommodation, or for the awarding of students' bursaries. So great is its influence that a good record of Komsomol work is considered along with the academic record when deciding which graduates will be given the best jobs.

As in the schools, the college Komsomols organize socially useful work among the students, but on a more ambitious scale, such as assisting with the harvest on collective farms, working on building sites for community projects, helping at Pioneer camps during the holidays, tutoring fellow-students who have difficulty with their work, and so on. Even major projects such as the building of the Leningrad Underground after the war owe a great deal to student labour organized in this way. Student branches also concern themselves with the conduct of other students, using meetings, discussions, and wall-newspapers to criticize the slackers and praise the conscientious.

One of the main attractions of Komsomol membership for some is the prospect of its leading, eventually, to membership of the Communist Party. It is debatable whether the ordinary Party member can exert much influence on policy, but for those aspiring to the leadership this is the only way up. There can be little doubt that the leaders exercise considerable power, at local as well as national level; for all the duties of membership (and the dangers, too, when times are troubled), admission to the 'corridors of power' is a great advantage to the ambitious in most walks of life. But it is extremely difficult to become a communist in the Soviet Union; so particular is the Party that all members and candidate members (probationers) total only four and a half per cent of the population. Political respectability is not enough; the aspiring member must prove his worth in work, study, and in voluntary effort of some kind for the common good. Even this, judging by the numbers, is not enough, but for anyone who seeks to climb the ladder of influence, a good record of active work in the Pioneers and the Komsomol is the best start he can have.

4. The Schools

After a period of almost continuous change during the late 1950s and most of the 1960s, the Soviet school has been relatively stable. The 'Khrushchov reforms' of 1958 were perhaps the most radical since the 1930s; but even before they had been fully implemented, there were clear signs that the authorities were having second thoughts about some points. In 1964, some important modifications were made (a few of them rather hastily), and in 1966 the Minister of Education announced the government's intention to make ten-year schooling universal by 1970, in one form or another. In the event, this proved rather optimistic, especially in the countryside, but in the towns the target was substantially met. In 1973, a new Basic Law on Education was passed, coming into effect from the beginning of 1974, but this was not another restructuring of the system. Essentially, it was a piece of consolidating legislation, confirming and developing the patterns that had become established since the beginning of the decade and before. Change, naturally, continues; there has been some rethinking of the approach to polytechnical education, and considerable attention is now being paid to the improvement of teaching methods, the adoption of modern techniques, and the search for ways of recognizing the diversity of the learners and their needs within an essentially unified system. More thought has been given to the problems of those at both ends of the process, namely the education of pre-school children and that of adults; and, appropriately at a time of increasing technological and social change, more is being made not only of further education and retraining, but of the whole concept of education as a lifelong process. The system continues to develop, but it is not expected that there will be any more drastic overhauls for some time.

The Present System

Pre-School Institutions

Pre-school education in the U.S.S.R. is neither compulsory nor available to all, nor is it free of charge. Nevertheless, it is expanding, and in some places can take in the majority of eligible children. Further, Soviet educationists increasingly stress the importance of expert pre-school guidance to the child's development. Accordingly, though they are not part of the compulsory system, these institutions can fittingly be included in an outline of the country's educational provision. They are of two kinds: nursery (*yasli*) for very young children, and kindergarten (*detski sad*) for children up to compulsory school age. Increasingly, the two types of institution are being organized together as nursery-kindergartens (*yaslie-sady*).

Nurseries normally accept children between the ages of six months and three years, and are often run by factories, offices, collective farms, and other enterprises for the children of their employees. Others are provided by the Ministry of Health and other public bodies. Most of these institutions, especially in the towns, operate all the year round, but some are organized on a seasonal basis; many collective farms find them necessary at, for example, harvest time, when the mothers are required in the fields, but do not provide them for the rest of the year. The functions of the nurseries are not primarily educational in the sense of providing any kind of formal instruction; they are more concerned with the physical welfare of the children, in seeing that they have healthy surroundings and medical care – doctors and nurses are usually on the staff – and with acting as institutionalized baby-sitters to release the mothers for work, thus taking over the traditional role of the *babushka* or grandmother in the Russian family. Apart from physical and medical care, the activities in the nursery consist largely of supervised play and rest. Teaching does not begin until the kindergarten stage.

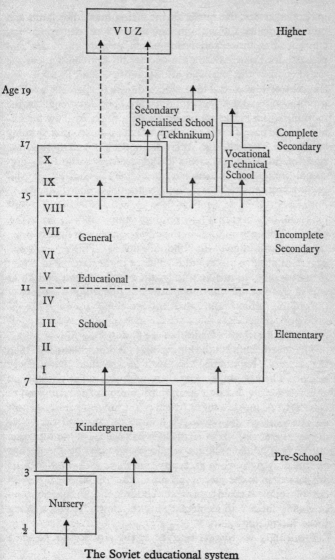

The Present System

Higher

VUZ

Age 19

Secondary
Specialised School
(Tekhnikum)

Complete
Secondary

Vocational
Technical
School

17

X

IX

15

VIII

VII   General

VI

V   Educational

11

IV

III   School

II

I

7

Incomplete
Secondary

Elementary

Kindergarten

Pre-School

3

Nursery

½

The Soviet educational system

The Schools

Kindergartens, like nurseries, are often provided by farms and industrial plants, though some are run by local departments of education; factories and farms which provide them are responsible for their maintenance and repair, but come under the jurisdiction of the local authorities, and are open to inspection and control. Hours tend to vary according to the parents' working conditions, but most kindergartens are open from eight in the morning to six in the evening, six days a week, to allow for differences in parents' shifts. Some children are boarders, going home only at weekends. Apart from doctors and nurses, the staffs of these establishments include teachers qualified in pre-school work; some of them have taken the full course at a pedagogic institute (a teacher training college of a higher standard), but most of them, as yet, have been trained at specialized secondary schools, where they have received a more modest, if relevant, preparation for the job. As in the nurseries, parents have to pay a fee as a contribution to the children's upkeep. This varies a good deal from place to place, and is adjusted to the parents' incomes; if the parents are unable to pay, their trade unions find all or part of the cost. The payment (which is to cover the expense of the children's food rather than the professional services) seems little discouragement; there are far more applicants for kindergartens and nurseries than there are places.

The 'curriculum' of the kindergarten is more methodical than the nursery programme, but much less so than the ordinary schools. The age range, from three to seven, is fairly wide, and children are divided into age groups (a rough approximation to classes) while they are there. Much of the time, as before, is spent on attending to the children's health, making sure they have plenty of exercise, fresh air, rest, a balanced diet, and medical attention. The children are regularly examined by the doctor, treatment is given when necessary, and those with severe defects are passed on to the special schools for the handicapped. A good deal of trouble is taken to make the children 'health conscious' by providing them with elementary health knowledge and training them in hygienic habits.

Elementary instruction is given in the artistic and, to some extent, in the academic field. There are drawing lessons of a rather formal and arid kind, but some free drawing is done as well, though there is much less of this than in a typical infant class in Britain; clay and plasticine are also used. Music lessons usually take the form of group singing, dancing, musical games, and so forth, but there is no attempt to deal with theory at this stage. The 'academic' side is, naturally, tackled at a very elementary level, and seeks to foster 'the understanding of the most elementary concepts in nature and in social life, the perfection of feeling and perception and the development of attentiveness, concept formation, thinking and language'. This is done through games and other activities, in which 'children are taught to observe, to compare, and to understand simple examples of the connection between cause and effect', such as noting the dependence of plants on moisture, warmth, and light, or the connection between temperature and the melting of ice or the freezing of water. They are taught to handle numbers by counting up to ten and doing simple oral arithmetic, and are familiarized with such concepts as equality and inequality, large and small, length and breadth; but formal functions are not introduced at this stage. It used to be the practice to start elementary reading and writing in the later stages of the kindergarten, but this has been discontinued; teachers in the first class in the ordinary school had to spend some time finding out how much their charges had learned, and then trying to bring the whole class to the same standard. This caused some problems: although some teachers claimed that they could iron out the differences within a couple of months (doubtless helped by the relatively regular conventions of Russian spelling), many more complained that the work of the kindergarten was ill coordinated with that of the school, and that they had to devote a good deal of attention to correcting bad learning habits. All too often, the formal work had been undertaken with more enthusiasm than skill (kindergarten teachers being rarely trained for this kind of work), but had not necessarily prepared the children adequately for school work.

Although it is stressed that preparation for entry to school is one of the important tasks of the whole kindergarten, this is clearly more pressing in the final years. Spoken language is given a great deal of attention, with particular emphasis on precision and correctness to make sure that 'children must be taught by the best examples of the mother tongue'; but fluency, expressiveness, and the development of vocabulary have their place too. As a preparation for literacy, children are taught to distinguish vowels from consonants, and palatalized from unpalatalized consonants (a basic distinction in Russian). But although children who have been taught in this way have been found to do better at school than those who have come in without such preparation, it is not intended that this should be overdone:

The pre-school child can learn much. But if he is to be well taught, it must not be forgotten that he is still little, that his powers are still limited, that he has a different emotional state of mind, and that he has strictly childlike needs and interests.[1]

Teachers in the Soviet Union, as elsewhere, are becoming increasingly convinced of the value of pre-school education. Quite apart from the convenience to the parents (the vast majority in the U.S.S.R. carry on working as a matter of course), it presents a unique opportunity for influencing the child's development – social, moral, aesthetic, even political – when he is at the most plastic stage. Great though the demand is, however, only a small majority receive any pre-school education, and only a minority – a large one, certainly – attend for more than two or three years. But numbers grow steadily. In permanent kindergartens alone, the number of places rose from just under four million in 1959 to over ten million by the 1970s; naturally, there are considerable variations from place to place – in some urban areas it is possible to provide for a majority.[2] It is clear, though, that it will be a long time before kindergartens are generally available for all children. Important though they are, pre-school institutions come below the ordinary schools and higher educational institutions on the list of priorities, and have to wait their turn for the available money and attention.

General Educational Schools (*Obshcheobrazovatel'nye shkoly*)

Soviet children enter the general schools on the first of September after their seventh birthday (*Pervoe sentyabrya* is something of a national festival) and stay on until they have completed at least eight years. The full course lasts for ten years, hence the popular name of *ten-year school* (*desyatiletnyaya shkola*).

Although the course is organized as a continuous process from the first to the tenth classes, elementary and secondary stages can be distinguished. The elementary stage comprises the first three classes, up to the age of about ten, during which the children are taught by a general class teacher for all subjects. At the secondary stage, from the fourth class onwards,[3] they are taught by subject specialists, though each form has a 'class adviser', one of the specialist teachers with the additional duty of keeping an eye on the welfare, progress and behaviour of the class in their school-work as a whole. The division into elementary and secondary stages is an organizational convenience, and does not imply any selection of the 'eleven-plus' type. As we shall see, some differentiation is possible after the eighth form, but up to that point the school is comprehensive and unstreamed throughout for all pupils, except for the very few who transfer to special or boarding schools.

Most pupils now take the entire general course in a single institution (over thirty-two million out of some forty-one million pupils in day schools are now enrolled in all-through ten-year schools*). There remain, however, some schools which provide only part of the course, and whose pupils have to move on to other schools to continue with the next stage. There are thus three types of general educational school (apart from those giving part-time courses):

(1) The *elementary school* (*nachal'naya shkola*) provides the first three classes as a rule, though there are still a few left which include the fourth class, usually in the more remote areas. Separate

* Figures are from *Narodnoe khozyaistvo SSSR v 1977 godu: Statisticheskii yezhegodnik* (Moscow, 1978).

elementary schools have been declining in numbers; there are now fewer than 44,000 of them, mostly very small (forty per cent of them have under forty pupils), and their total enrolment is under one million.

(2) The *incomplete secondary school* (*nepolnaya srednyaya shkola*) provides the first eight classes (about age seven to fifteen); they are also known as eight-year schools. These are a good deal more common; there are at present about 46,000 of them, with nearly eight million pupils. Separate eight-year schools have also been dwindling in number, though less drastically than the elementary.

(3) The *complete secondary school* (*polnaya srednyaya shkola*) provides the entire ten-year course. There are nearly 53,000 of these. Most pupils now stay in schools of this type for their entire school careers, though there is a change-over for some after the eighth class, when some go off to other types of institution, while others come in from eight-year schools. Confusingly enough, when Soviet sources mention 'secondary schools', they refer to the entire ten-year school, not only to the senior classes.

In the fifth form a foreign language is introduced for all children. Most schools offer only one; English is the most usual, with French, German, and Spanish following behind. In keeping with recent declarations on the need to improve conversational fluency, classes are divided for language teaching into groups of twenty or less (a typical class numbers thirty to forty pupils).[4] This, at least, is the general idea, but it is not always done. There is still a shortage of language teachers, and the quality of teaching, for all the official uniformity of method, varies from the admirable to the dull and ineffective. A number of experimental schools begin languages earlier, in the second form or even before, and teach other subjects in that language as soon as possible thereafter. Most of them are English, French, or German schools, but there are a few using Chinese, Arabic, Hindi, Swahili, and other less familiar languages. Language schools appear to be popular with parents – applications always exceed the number of places. They are expanding,[5] but more slowly than most people would like, mainly due to the particular shortage of teachers capable of teaching history or physics in English or French, to say nothing of Chinese or Arabic.

The curriculum of the general school is academic in content, with special emphasis on the scientific subjects, starting with a narrow range of subjects and broadening out as the course progresses. Under the latest scheme (see Table), the time is spent on Russian (twelve hours), mathematics (six), physical education and work study (two hours each), and one hour each on music and drawing. The programme is not quite as narrow as it looks, for the term 'Russian' can cover as wide a field in Russian schools as 'English' does in ours. By the time the pupils are in their

Ten-Year School Syllabus[6]

Subjects:	Hours per week in classes:									
	I	II	III	IV	V	VI	VII	VIII	IX	X
1. Russian language	12	11	10	6	6	4	3	2	—	—
2. Literature	—	—	—	2	2	2	2	3	4	3
3. Mathematics	6	6	6	6	6	6	6	6	5	5
4. History	—	—	—	2	2	2	2	3	4	3
5. Soviet govt. & law	—	—	—	—	—	—	—	1	—	—
6. Social study	—	—	—	—	—	—	—	—	—	2
7. Nature study	—	1	2	2	—	—	—	—	—	—
8. Geography	—	—	—	—	2	3	2	2	2	—
9. Biology	—	—	—	—	2	2	2	2	1	2
10. Physics	—	—	—	—	—	2	2	3	4	5
11. Astronomy	—	—	—	—	—	—	—	—	—	1
12. Technical drawing	—	—	—	—	—	—	1	1	1	—
13. Chemistry	—	—	—	—	—	—	2	2	3	3
14. Foreign language	—	—	—	—	4	3	3	2	2	2
15. Art	1	1	1	1	1	1	—	—	—	—
16. Music	1	1	1	1	1	1	1	—	—	—
17. Physical education	2	2	2	2	2	2	2	2	2	2
18. Labour training	2	2	2	2	2	2	2	2	2	2
19. Pre-military trng.	—	—	—	—	—	—	—	—	2	2
Total	24	24	24	24	30	30	30	31	32	32
20. Work practice (days)	—	—	—	—	5	5	5	—	22	—
21. Optional studies	—	—	—	—	—	—	2	3	4	4

eighth year, they are attending for thirty-one hours a week, the time being spent thus: five hours of Russian language and literature, six of mathematics, two of history, one of technical drawing, three of physics, and two each of geography, biology, chemistry, foreign language, physical education, and work training. Three hours are also set aside for optional studies. There are some minor variations where conditions require; in physical education, for example, ski-ing is compulsory from the third form, but where climatic conditions make this impossible the time is allocated to gymnastics, athletics, and games such as volleyball and basketball. But apart from minor departures of this kind, the basic pattern remains.[7] Moral education is not separately timetabled, but introduced, as we have seen, through the medium of other subjects.

Work-training has had its ups and downs in the last few years, but remains an important element in the school. It begins in the first form with simple lessons in the manipulation of tools and materials – sewing, modelling, paper-cutting, etc. Carpentry with allied skills is introduced in the fourth form, and various mechanical skills are added later. There is less manual training of this kind for girls, who spend some of their time in the higher forms on the group of activities variously described as 'domestic science', 'homecraft', 'domestic economy', or something such, including needlework, cookery, home management, and so forth. But the girls do receive technical training as well, while the boys appear to have some 'domestic' instruction along with their other practical work. The difference of degree of time spent on industrial and domestic skills is practically the only concession made by the Soviet school to sexual differences. The fact that the girls will almost certainly be workers *as well as* wives and mothers doubtless has something to do with it.

At the incomplete secondary stage, there is no attempt to prepare the pupils for any particular occupation; the training is polytechnical, not vocational. By the end of the eighth form, they have all had some experience of woodwork and metalwork, and of machine tools as well as hand tools; they have had practice in the care of plants and animals on the school plots or on visits to collective farms (or on their own farms in the case of rural schools); more important, they have had instruction on the relevance of scientific theory to its practical use in industry and agriculture. Also, during the secondary stage, they have visited (and in some cases done some work in) different kinds of industrial and agricultural enterprises. But this is as far as it goes; direct trade training comes, if at all, at a later stage.

The curriculum described here is, of course, for children whose mother tongue is Russian. In schools for children of other nationalities, teaching is carried out in the national languages, Russian normally being introduced at the beginning of the course.[8] In many of the minority republics there are sizeable numbers of Russian residents, whose children can go to Russian-language schools;[9] these are just like those of the R.S.F.S.R., except that they have to learn in addition Armenian, Georgian, Uzbek, or whatever the language of the republic concerned happens to be – much to the annoyance of many Russian parents living temporarily in the area, faced with the prospect of their children having to tackle two or three new languages in turn as their appointments shift from place to place. In other respects, the curriculum of the non-Russian schools is much the same, including a foreign (i.e. non-Soviet) language.

The policy of providing medical attention is continued in the general school. Each has a doctor and a nurse on the staff, though these may be shared with another school. Their duties, apart from on-the-spot treatment, include talks on health and hygiene to pupils and parents, conducting regular medical inspections, and arranging for inspection by dentists and medical specialists as well. The children are also X-rayed every session. As the cities are much better off for doctors than the countryside, it is likely that the rural schools have considerable difficulty in keeping such an ambitious programme going.

Class instruction is supplemented by homework, which can be a heavy burden at times. In theory, homework is limited to one hour a night in the elementary classes, and two in the secondary. In practice, this is exceeded in many cases, especially in the upper forms. This is due partly to lack of coordination between subject specialists – a familiar enough phenomenon in this country – although a record is supposed to be kept; it is also due in some cases to over-optimistic estimates of what can reasonably be expected in the time. Certainly, there are frequent complaints in the educational press and *Family and School*. One attempt to improve the situation is the organization by some schools of supervised homework sessions on the premises.

It is at the eight-year stage that the Pioneer Organization does most of its work. Every school is supposed to have a Pioneer room for extra-curricular activities; these, as might be expected, range from the ample, through the barely adequate to the downright meagre. Moreover, there is still a shortage of buildings, so that some of the schools still work on a shift system, the younger classes coming in the morning and the older ones in the afternoon. Although the children are, as a result, free for other activities, the school premises and many of the teaching staff may not be available. There are, of course, the Pioneer Palaces and Houses, but it is generally felt that a close link should be kept between the school and non-scholastic activities, which is one reason why the authorities are anxious to do away with the remnants of schooling by shifts.

Unlike the nursery and kindergarten, the general school is both free and compulsory. Parents, however, do have to pay for their children's materials and uniforms. Textbooks, which formerly had to be bought by the parents, are now provided free. If they are unable to afford the expense, they can have these things provided free, and the cost is met from a fund administered by the Parents' Committee; the same applies to meal vouchers for the dining-room. As for uniforms, many parents prefer to make these themselves, getting the patterns free from the schools. Clothes are generally expensive in the Soviet Union, but the price of children's clothes is low in comparison. They are also becoming more attractive, both to children and parents. The rather military-looking boys' outfit, complete with button-up tunic and peaked cap, was replaced by a plain suit and beret in 1963, but the girls were left with the antiquated (and hideous) dark brown serge dress, with frilly collars and cuffs and black aprons for ordinary days, white ones for special occasions. This is now vanishing, totally unregretted, and being replaced by a navy-blue pinafore dress for the younger girls and a navy skirt, blazer, blouse, and beret outfit for senior girls. It is generally accepted that uniforms as such can have a 'democratizing' effect, but that this need no longer mean dressing the boys like pupils of a military academy or the girls like the inmates of a school for young ladies of Tsarist times.

Strictly speaking, compulsory schooling ends after the eighth class, and a few do leave then to take up regular jobs. In the early 1960s a large minority did so, but in 1966 it was decided to extend complete secondary schooling, in one form or another, to include all young people in the country; the process was to be 'substantially' complete by 1970–71.[10] In the event, this target was reached quickly in the towns, but took rather longer to attain in the countryside; even now, it is doubtful if all those expected to continue their secondary general schooling (while training for a trade, for example) in fact do so, and there is evidence that some youngsters still manage to leave even before they are legally supposed to. Nevertheless, the goal of complete secondary schooling for all is at least in sight. It was not intended that all should necessarily go on to finish the full-time general ten-year school. After the eighth class, there remain different types of school, offering various combinations of general education and vocational training.

The main choices for further schooling after the eighth form can be classified as follows:

(a) The upper forms (IX and X) of the ten-year school. This is now the preferred course, with about sixty per cent on average going on. According to the Minister of Education[11] this figure is expected to rise to seventy-five per cent of the age-group; the rest will continue to leave for other kinds of institution where their particular interests are more directly catered for.

The greater part of the students' time is spent on general educational subjects – Russian, mathematics, history, geography, social study, biology, physics, chemistry, astronomy, foreign language, and physical education being compulsory for all students. In addition, six hours a week are now set aside for optional studies, giving the students the chance to specialize further or broaden their curriculum in school time if they so wish.[12]

Work-training, both theoretical and practical, figures more largely than in the eight-year school. Under the reforms of 1958, this took up about a third of the entire course. Some of it was carried out in the schools' own workshops, experimental plots, etc., but most of it took place outside the school. Usually, it was geared to a particular occupation – machine-tooling, lathe-operating, and so forth, and most of it was carried out in the appropriate factory. The students of Moscow School No. 273, for example, did their practical work in the Severyanin Engineering Factory; those of Leningrad School No. 289 in the local rubber-tyre plant; Kiev School No. 72 in the Krasny Excavator Factory; and similar arrangements existed between schools in country districts and the collective farms. An extra year was added to the course to provide the extra time required.

In 1964, however, after frequent complaints about the time-wasting nature of much of this production practice (both from the point of view of the students and the factory managements), substantial cuts were introduced. Under the scheme[13] now being introduced, work-training has been brought down to a basic course in polytechnical theory and practice of four hours a week, taught chiefly in the school workshops. Production training in factories is to continue only where adequate facilities exist. According to the Soviet Minister of Education,[14] about a third of the schools in the R.S.F.S.R. intend to continue with this; the rest will confine themselves to the more general polytechnical course, with extended periods of practice only in the ninth class.

At the end of the tenth form, students can take the secondary school certificate or 'Attestation of Maturity' (*attestat zrelosti*), roughly comparable to the G.C.E.[15] This entitles them to apply for admission to institutes of higher education; but it does not guarantee entry – a preliminary examination must still be taken by all applicants.

(b) *Secondary Specialized Schools* (*Srednie spetsial'nye uchebnye zavedeniya*). These offer a combination of general and vocational education; the vocational element predominates, with about twice as much time as the general. Between three and four hundred occupations are catered for in these schools.[16] They fall into many different categories, but two broad types can be distinguished: a *tekhnikum* deals with highly skilled technical or clerical jobs, an *uchilishche* with occupations of the sort sometimes described as 'semi-professional'. There are *tekhnikumy*, for instance, with courses in electronics, engineering, electromechanics, transport, communications, construction, textiles, metallurgy, chemical engineering, and a host of others in light and heavy industry; in agriculture, forestry, fisheries, soil science, food processing; and in economics, management, finance, book-keeping and clerical work. *Uchilishcha* also cover a wide range, but the commonest are medical (for nurses, pharmacists, health-workers, and the like), and the artistic and cultural schools, which train librarians and cultural organizers, and give courses in music and the visual arts. Many pre-school and elementary teachers still receive their training in schools of this type, the *Pedagogic Schools* (*pedagogicheskie uchilishcha*); the aim of the authorities is to have them all go through a college course, like the rest of their colleagues, as soon as possible, but since teacher supply is still something of a problem, it has not been found possible to dispense with the pedagogic schools yet.

As well as the professional qualifications, students in secondary specialized schools can take the certificate of secondary education, and are eligible to apply for admission to higher educational institutions; the vocational bias of the school does not necessarily commit them to the job, but serves to familiarize them with practical work, gives a professional qualification to those not proceeding to higher levels, and provides a second string for the bow of the student who fails to get into college and a basis of practical experience for the one who does. The majority, however, go straight into the appropriate jobs on completion of their courses.

Students who have come directly from the eighth form study for about three or four years, according to their speciality; two-year courses, with a much greater emphasis on the vocational

The Schools

side, are also provided for those who have completed a full secondary education elsewhere. Some of the specialized schools come under the republic Ministries of Agriculture, Public Health, Culture and the like, but for the most part they are the responsibility of the U.S.S.R. Ministry of Higher and Secondary Specialized Education and its republican counterparts, unlike the general secondary schools, which come under the jurisdiction of the Ministries of Education.

(c) *Vocational Technical Schools* (*Professional'no-teckhnicheskie uchilishcha*). These are sometimes referred to as 'trade schools' or by the old name of 'labour-reserve schools'. They are much more specialized than the other two types described so far; the main emphasis is on learning a particular trade. General subjects are limited to between fifteen and twenty per cent of the time, the rest being spent in field or workshop. Courses last for between six months and three years, depending on the trade involved (about eight hundred different occupations are dealt with) and students are paid at apprentice rates. The course culminates with the award of a trade diploma. It is theoretically possible to go on from these schools to higher education, but to do so the student will have to eke out the rather meagre amount of general education. Some in fact go to polytechnical institutes and the like, later, after studying in continuation courses in their spare time, but most students with their eyes on a college place will prefer to carry on with ten-year schooling, the simplest and most direct way to the higher levels.

Administratively, these schools are separate from the rest of the educational system, and come under the jurisdiction of the State Committee of the U.S.S.R. Council of Ministers on Vocational-Technical Education. Training for many less highly skilled trades is still given 'on the job', not in a school, but the present trend is towards having more and more skills catered for in the vocational technical schools.

(d) *Part-time Schools*. General secondary and secondary specialized schooling can be had on a part-time as well as a full-time basis. These may take the form of *evening and shift secondary general educational schools* (*vechernie i smennye srednie obshcheo-*

98

brazovatel'nye shkoly), sometimes still referred to as 'Schools for Working Youth' or 'Schools for Rural Youth', and are intended for young people who for some reason did not continue with full-time education after the age of fifteen. Students normally attend in the evenings if they live in the towns, although such schools may be organized on a seasonal basis in the country, and correspondence courses are available for those living in remote areas. Most secondary specialized schools have *evening and external departments* (*vechernie i zaochnye otdeleniya*), and there are forty-five *external secondary specialized schools* (*zaochnye srednie spetsial'nye uchebnye zavedeniya*) which specialize in providing courses of this kind.[17] Although the range of courses available part-time is not quite as extensive as in full-time schools, the content of the curricula is much the same.

After 1958, there was a great increase in the number of students following part-time courses; and in 1964, when some of Khrushchov's policies were partially reversed in other respects, these courses were still seen as an important part of the system.[18] This is likely to continue in the case of secondary specialized courses. With the present drive towards obligatory ten-year schooling, the importance of part-time general courses is likely to decline; in marked contrast to the pronouncements of the Khrushchov era, the authorities have expressed a clear preference for full-time study if possible.[19] In two fields, however, part-time courses are likely to have a continuing part to play. One is in the remote areas, where it will be a long time before full-time facilities even approach those of the towns and larger villages. The other concerns students in vocational–technical schools; trade-training does not, apparently, count as full secondary education, and students who take this road will have to make up the general educational side on a part-time basis.[20]

In theory, it is possible to go on from any kind of secondary school to higher education, but it is clear that students who have continued in the ten-year school will have a better chance than others, in view of the fierce competition for entry to the colleges and universities. The Soviet authorities claim that it is entirely a matter of free choice what kind of secondary school a

99

The Schools

pupil enters, so that no general selective procedure is necessary. It does seem that any pupil who wishes to continue in the general school can do so; indeed, a common complaint is that the targets for numbers going on from the eighth to the ninth form have not been met in the rural areas.[21] The problem is not, therefore, shortage of places in the upper forms, but rather shortage of students, given the ambitious targets that have been set. Secondary specialized schools are another matter. Offering as they do professional qualifications as well as a general secondary certificate, they are increasingly popular, so much so in many cases that some kind of selection has to be used. In Leningrad, for example, schools offering courses in computer programming or electronics are inundated with applications, ten for every place. When this happens, selection is by competitive examination, taking into account the cumulative record of the applicant's work and conduct that has followed him all the way through the eight-year school.

Special Schools and Boarding Schools

So far we have been concerned with the schools attended by the great majority of Soviet schoolchildren. Side by side with the ordinary system, however, there are some schools that take in specially selected groups of children, for one reason or another. These include schools that offer a special course significantly different from the ordinary establishments, and the large number of boarding schools.

Special Schools

These are of three main types: (a) special schools for the handicapped; (b) army and navy cadet schools; (c) schools for the artistically gifted.

(a) *Special Schools for the Handicapped*. Special schools for physically and mentally handicapped children are classified according to the seriousness of the cases; whereas the Ministries of Education are responsible for those dealing with children who can be trained, more serious cases, such as cripples and those

100

suffering from congenital defects, go to schools run by the Ministries of Public Health, while the really hopeless ones, such as congenital idiots, cretins, and the like, are cared for in institutions under the authority of the Ministries of Public Insurance.

There are special schools for the blind and partially sighted children, the deaf and partially hearing, the deaf and dumb, children suffering from serious speech defects, children with brain damage and brain disease, the emotionally and psychologically disturbed, and so forth. Many of these institutions are residential, but some function as day schools. The work done is partly remedial – exercises for the improvement of speech, for example – and partly compensatory, such as training blind children in the use of braille lettering and teaching them work-skills that lie within their compass. As far as possible, the normal school curriculum is used, even with the mentally retarded, and only departed from or slowed down with reluctance, if the children really cannot cope. It is in keeping with the Soviet suspicion (but not total rejection) of the idea of innate intelligence that cases of mental backwardness are usually attributed to some kind of brain damage; mental and physical defects are regarded as different aspects of the same thing. Intelligence tests and similar devices are not, of course, used at all. Children are sent to schools for the mentally defective on the basis of observation, at school or kindergarten, over a period of up to one year. Special schools include 'forest' convalescent schools, where children in delicate health or suffering from such diseases as tuberculosis can receive general education combined with medical care, and can have the advantages of fresh air and good climatic conditions to help their recovery.

Special schools for the handicapped are staffed by nurses, doctors, pediatricians, and teachers who have taken courses in 'defectology' in the pedagogic institutes. These schools also have the usual Pioneer organizations, and Parents' Committees function where possible, though this can rarely be managed where the schools are far from the parents' homes, as are the forest schools and some of the boarding establishments. Most visitors report that the atmosphere in the handicapped schools is more relaxed than in the ordinary ones, with much less pressure on the children and much greater allowances made for their inability to cope with the work. Generally, the object is to remedy the deficiencies if this can be done at all, and to pursue the children's intellectual, polytechnical, and moral education as far as possible if it cannot.

(b) *Military Cadet Schools*. These are normally ten-year boarding schools for general education which prepare cadets for the Soviet armed forces. There are two kinds: *Suvorov Schools* for the army and air force, and *Nakhimov Schools* for the navy. Founded in 1943, they were originally intended for the orphans of military personnel who had been killed in the Second World War. At the present time, children, especially orphans, of members of the armed forces are given preference. Otherwise entry is by competitive examination. Apart from military and naval studies, ranging from small-arms handling and barrack-square drill to tactics and strategy, the course is much the same as in the ordinary schools.

(c) *Schools for the Artistically Gifted*. As a marked exception in an otherwise comprehensive system, the U.S.S.R. has a number of special schools for children who show a high level of talent in one of the fine arts, such as music, drama, ballet, painting and sculpture, and so forth. There are not many of these – there are only about fifty special art schools in the country, for example, and sixteen ballet schools.[22] The standard of work is high throughout, and some of them, like the Kirov Ballet School in Leningrad, have produced world-renowned figures in their fields. Places are filled by competition among children from the ordinary schools, normally at the end of the first year, although entry can take place for two or three years after that. There also appears to be a certain amount of talent-spotting; certainly an official of the Kirov School regularly goes round the dancing clubs of the eight-year schools looking for likely candidates. Many of these institutions have survived, in one form or another, since Tsarist times, and have been retained and extended under the Soviet system because of the veneration for the arts in Russian tradition and communist theory alike.

The curriculum of these schools is devoted partly to general educational subjects, as in the ordinary schools, and the rest to the particular art involved. 'Work-training', as found in other schools, does not figure here; the artistic activity itself counts as 'labour' in the case of these specialists – nobody pretends that their contribution to the good of Soviet society is less than any number of engineers. Further, there is the practical consideration that for the future concert violinist or ballerina, working with lathe or welding-torch is unlikely to be beneficial, and may well be dangerous.

When Khrushchov issued his memorandum on 'Strengthening the Ties of the School with Life' in 1958, one of his proposals was to extend the system of special schools for the gifted to include scientists as well as artists. 'It may be found expedient,' he said, 'to pick from among capable pupils at the existing schools particularly gifted children showing, for instance, an aptitude for physics, mathematics, biology, draughtsmanship, etc., and collect them together at certain schools.'[23] This suggestion had a very mixed reception. For a couple of months the issue was debated, sometimes hotly, in the pages of *Pravda*, *Uchitel'skaya gazeta*, and elsewhere.[24] The main line of attack was that such a step would be an undesirable departure from the comprehensive principle, and that it was unnecessary anyway. The special art schools, long established and familiar as they were, were felt to be a special case, whereas special treatment for the gifted in other fields was resisted as a form of segregation. In some quarters, too, there seemed to be a suspicion that the setting up of new categories of special schools might provide an easy open door for the children of influential parents. Whatever the reasons for the opposition, this particular proposal was quietly dropped when the law on educational reform was finally published.

Since then, however, special schools for *older* children exceptionally gifted in mathematics have been making their appearance. A secondary boarding school for such pupils was set up at Akademgorodok in Novosibirsk in 1963,[25] drawing its pupils from the winners of the nationwide competition or 'Olympiad'[26] in mathematics and physics. Since then, similar schools have been opened in Moscow, Kiev, and Leningrad. Compromise solutions of this kind, and the increasing emphasis on time for optional studies in the senior forms of the general schools, suggest that the authorities are trying to get the best of both worlds by combining unified early schooling with more differentiation later. Clearly, the problem of what to do with the highly gifted child in a comprehensive context still remains. Schools of this kind, even for older pupils, are undoubtedly a departure from the comprehensive principle of the system. But three considerations make them less objectionable to the doubters than they would otherwise be: firstly, there are far too few of them to 'cream off' the ordinary schools; secondly, they cater for *specific* talents, not for gifted children generally; finally, and probably most importantly, their existence does not relegate the ordinary schools to inferior status. The normal route to further and higher education remains the ten-year general school.

Boarding Schools

The Soviet boarding school (*shkola internat*) was called into being by a resolution of the Twentieth Congress of the Communist Party in 1956. Numbers expanded rapidly, until by 1965 over two and a half million pupils were enrolled in such schools.[27]

The boarding school curriculum does not differ fundamentally from that of the day schools. There are some differences, due to the fact that the children spend the entire day there. All of them have supervised homework sessions, which result in the work being done in less time than by children living at home. Some find it possible to continue subjects like music and drawing all through the course; others set aside one day a week for excursions, making up the time for regular studies during the rest of the week; others, such as Moscow No. 12 and Kaluga No. 2, use a system of lengthened periods to make more practical work possible. For the most part, however, they do not significantly differ, in formal teaching or in the qualifications they can provide, from their day-school counterparts.

These schools are not in any sense special schools for an *élite*, in spite of misleading analogies sometimes drawn with the so-called 'public' schools in England. Rather the reverse; there is a system of priorities for entry, which gives preference to orphans, the children of widows and unmarried mothers, invalids, children from large or overcrowded families, and so forth. There are cases, too, of temporary enrolments: one hears of children admitted during their mother's absence in hospital, returning to the day schools on her recovery; or of children, originally admitted because their homes were overcrowded, being withdrawn by their parents when they got a new and bigger flat. Sometimes children are taken in from homes where the parents have difficulty in controlling them. On the whole, they tend to have a higher proportion of deprived or problem children than the day schools, so that the academic standards are sometimes lower. Nevertheless, competition for entry is keen, especially in areas where the housing shortage is particularly acute.

Although instruction is of course free, parents may be charged a fee as a contribution towards the children's board and lodging; this is adjusted according to parental income, the maximum contribution being twenty per cent of the economic cost. Very few in fact pay as much as this, since most children have been admitted on the grounds of some kind of disadvantage in the first place. At least a quarter pay nothing at all.[28]

Children live in the school from Monday to Saturday, going home (if they have one) on Sundays and during school holidays. The authorities insist that the schools maintain as close links as possible with the children's homes, and pour scorn on the idea that they are trying to drive a wedge between the children and their parents. As in the day schools, Parents' Committees are active, and individual parents are encouraged to visit the school and discuss problems with the staff. Children are released to go home for family occasions, such as weddings and funerals; this causes some inconvenience, it is said, but it is felt to be important to keep up the child's contact with his family. Organizers of boarding schools say that the family and the school help each other in the child's upbringing, and clearly feel that the family gains more from the exchange.

Discipline in the boarding schools is usually more strict than elsewhere. Many of the children have been unused to regular meal-hours and bedtimes, adequate fresh air and exercise; to put this right, the school has to make regulations on such matters, and enforce them if persuasion is not enough. As in the day schools, the sexes are mixed; this is said to be a further reason for supervision in the case of the older pupils, but it is not felt that there is anything odd or undesirable in mixed boarding as such. According to one director, anxious that the school should not become a self-contained community cut off from society at large, it is important that the sexes should be taught together, *especially* in boarding schools.

There can be little doubt that the boarding school is popular with parents, if only for practical reasons; the constant flood of applications makes this clear enough. Many teachers, too, are convinced that it offers several practical advantages. It is usually possible to provide more extra-curricular activities than in the ordinary schools; it is easier to modify the timetable; there is nearly always more room and opportunity for sport; a boarding establishment offers more scope for 'socially useful labour' in kitchen, dormitories, and grounds, as well as classrooms. Most important of all, since the children live there all the time, they can be more readily organized as a 'collective', whose influence is more immediate, more continuous, less subject to interference than that of the day school. The boarding school, in short, is regarded by many Soviet teachers as more promising ground for social and moral education in the widest sense.

Few, however, claim that the system is devoid of drawbacks. The children are together *all* the time, privacy is difficult or impossible, and living in the school atmosphere twenty-four hours a day can become oppressive. Some teachers are little concerned about this, pointing out that for children from overcrowded homes privacy is an unknown luxury anyway, that children generally like to be with their own crowd, that going home for weekends and holidays provides an adequate break from the school environment, and that boarding schools are just as much the schools of the locality as are the day schools. (Most of the boarding schools are in the towns, not tucked away in the countryside; Moscow alone has over seventy. But others are less sure; in Boarding School No. 15 in Moscow, for instance, deliberate steps are taken to vary the children's surroundings by getting them away from the school at regular and frequent intervals. Every Thursday, the elementary classes are taken, by teachers or older pupils, to zoos, parks, museums, sports clubs, and on visits to other schools. Semi-official trips are also encouraged; some boys from this school went recently to the diving championships at Minsk, others who had made some money by spare-time work bought motor-cycles and went off on their own, touring the Ukraine and the Caucasus; even some of the smaller children have been on camping excursions in the forests. Most directors, it seems, are determined that the boarding school will not become a closed community cut off from the outside world. Although they have been functioning now for more than a decade, one gains the impression that the boarding schools are still regarded by the authorities as partly experimental, and that the directors are accordingly given rather more freedom of action than is normal in the school system at large.

Apart from teachers, doctors, and nurses, the boarding schools have on their staffs so-called 'upbringers'[29] (*vospitateli*) who act as helpers; they are lower-paid than teachers and hold lesser qualifications. Broadly, their duties are to concern themselves with the physical and moral welfare of the children, organize sport and extra-curricular activities, supervision of meals and dormitories, and much of the administration of school activities, but not class teaching. As a rule, none of the staff (apart from a matron) live in the school; class tutors and *vospitateli*, however, take it in turn to sleep in, two at a time, which works out in practice at about once or twice a month.

Physical conditions vary a good deal; on the whole, living accommodation appears to be adequate and clean but rather cramped. Some boarding schools were hastily converted from day schools shortly after the directive of 1956; these are usually the most crowded, as space was often lacking for the building of suitable extensions. Others are more spacious: Moscow No. 7 is a large five-storey building in a park, Moscow No. 15 has two buildings, one for normal schoolwork and one for dormitories and dining-room, though there too the dormitories are crowded and storage space extremely limited. Building progress is obviously having difficulty in coping with demand.

A modified version of the boarding school is the 'prolonged-day school' (*shkola prodlennogo dnya*). Pupils come to these schools in the morning for lessons and stay on for the afternoon and early evening, when the time is occupied with club and Pioneer activities, homework supervision, organized walks and rambles, and the like. The children also eat there, returning home about seven o'clock after the evening meal. Such schools are expanding, and are proving even more popular; they offer working parents many of the practical advantages of boarding schools without going to the length of having the children live away from home.

When boarding schools were first introduced, there were many indications that the authorities intended to make them, eventually, the regular form of general education for all Soviet children. This may have been the intention, but now it is clear that this idea has been dropped. The usual line taken by officials is that the expansion of boarding and prolonged-day schools will continue but that there is no intention of replacing the day schools. As for suggestions that the family is being undermined, they point to the elaborate efforts being made, in day and boarding schools alike, to secure the active cooperation of the parents in their children's education.

There are many possible reasons for this change of policy. For one thing, boarding schools, even with parental contributions, are a greater strain on the economy. Boarding school places cost the state over seven times as much as day school places,[30] and although government spending on education is high in the U.S.S.R., there are more pressing claims on it. Further, high though the demand is at the moment, there is little evidence that the majority of parents would welcome the idea. Doubtless most of them could be persuaded or cajoled into acceptance, but we have seen that the authorities attach great value to the cooperation of parents with the school; loss of this would be too high a price to pay for whatever advantages might be gained by general boarding, even if the country could afford it. Also, there is the feeling in many quarters that although boarding education may be highly suitable for some children, there is no evidence that it would be universally desirable, even in principle.

Predictions can be hazardous, especially when they are made about the Soviet Union, but it does seem clear that the boarding school has come to stay. It is unlikely to replace the day school; and as for suggestions that it might develop into a special school for the privileged, on the English pattern, this seems, on the basis of the present methods of selection for entry, equally unlikely.

Reforms and Reappraisals

Before Khrushchov began the prolonged shake-up of the Soviet school system, the great majority of Soviet children received the bulk of their schooling in general schools of three types: *four-year* or *elementary* schools, from the ages of seven to eleven; *seven-year* or *incomplete secondary* schools, from seven to fourteen; and *ten-year* or *complete secondary* schools, from seven to seventeen. These all offered the same courses; there was no difference in the curriculum or the standard of teaching, only in the stages reached.

The *four-year* schools were found only in remote areas. At one time there were some places where this was the only available schooling, but it was claimed that this state of affairs had ceased long before 1958. On completion of the four-year course, all children went on to the nearest seven-year school to pursue their studies from where they had left off.

In 1958, the *seven-year* school was still the standard in most areas, and for most children was the end of their general education; many could, and did, go on to a ten-year school, but since this often meant a move to the nearest town, many pupils dropped out at fourteen.

The *ten-year* school was the most complete form of general schooling. From the age of seven to eleven, children were taught by one class teacher, and by specialists thereafter. There was no break at eleven or twelve, as happens in this country, the primary and secondary stages being organized in the same school. The curriculum was identical with the four- and seven-year schools, but was taken further to the point of the Attestation of Maturity. Like the other forms of general school, it was co-educational, un-streamed and comprehensive throughout. The course was highly formal and academic, more so than at present, and gave little or no choice of subjects. In the first form, there were thirteen hours of instruction in Russian language and literature, six in mathematics, two in physical education, one each in singing and drawing, and one in socially useful labour. The next two years saw little change, but in the fourth form history, geography, and biology made their appearance with two hours each. In the fifth form specialist teaching began, and a foreign language, usually English or German, was introduced with four hours a week. Drawing and singing vanished as regular school subjects after the sixth form, and others were brought in, until the tenth-form timetable looked like this: four hours per week of Russian language and literature, six of mathematics, four of history, one of the Constitution of the U.S.S.R., four of physics, one of astronomy, four of chemistry, one of psychology, three of the foreign language, three of physical education, one of technical drawing, two of 'fundamentals of production' – that is, practice in agriculture, machine study, electrical equipment, and the like. Biology and geography had dropped out at the end of the ninth form. There was also provision for excursions of various kinds, later extended to include some practical work experience. Even with this, however, the school's work was overwhelmingly academic, closely geared to the needs of higher education, and this was the kind of course that most children had to undergo.

Vocational schools were a mixed category, including the *tekhni-kumy* and other specialized secondary schools, 'labour-reserve' or trade schools, and so on. Some of these catered for the graduates of ten-year schools, but for the most part they were courses with a vocational bias that filled in between the seven-year school and full-time work. The courses varied greatly in length from five years to two years or less.[31] The various types of *special schools* also existed alongside the ordinary system.

The change from this state of affairs could hardly be described as a bombshell. Change had been in the air for some time; as far back as the Nineteenth Congress of the Communist Party in 1952 there had been some hints about the desirability of reviving the polytechnical idea. Discussion mounted slowly from then onwards, until at the Twentieth Congress in 1956 Khrushchov criticized the schools for being 'divorced from life', and observed that 'those who finish school are insufficiently prepared for practical work'. This theme was heard frequently and in more detail over the next two years, culminating in Khrushchov's memorandum of September 1958, entitled 'Strengthening the Ties of the School with Life, and Further Developing the System of Public Education'. More discussion followed, but Khrushchov's criticisms and proposals, with some adjustments, formed the basis for the declaration of the Central Committee of the Party on the subject and finally, in December, for the law reforming the Soviet educational system.

The most significant changes were, among others, the increase of compulsory schooling from seven to eight years. Instead of introducing universal ten-year schooling, however, as had originally been intended, the reforms concentrated on providing a wider range of choice after the eight-year school – part-time schools, vocational technical schools, secondary specialized schools, and 'secondary general educational labour polytechnical schools with production training'; courses in these last were increased by one year to accommodate the extra time needed for practical work, as we have seen. Indeed, the retreat from the overwhelmingly academic character of the old ten-year school, and the stress on practical work for all, was the keynote of the 1958 reforms. The reasons for this were not entirely educational; economic, practical, and socio-political factors were at work as well.

Among the practical considerations were the shortage of manpower and the economic cost that would have been involved in universal ten-year schooling at that time. Soviet economic planning was geared to large-scale defence and research expenditure, a high rate of industrial expansion, and a substantial increase in

housing and consumer goods. Even the partial success of this
policy required, among other things, a highly skilled labour force;
but as it was, the ravages of war were still making themselves felt
in the form of a drastically lowered birth-rate (together with the
loss of children in the occupied areas) during the war years.[32] This
seriously reduced the numbers available for the various branches
of industrial production, and keeping all young people in full-
time schooling till the age of seventeen, especially schooling of an
academic and non-practical nature, would have aggravated an
already serious problem. From this point of view, the 1958 reforms were an attempt to extend secondary education and meet
the needs of industry at the same time.

It had also been felt for some time that the ten-year schools,
successful in their own way though they were, had become too
narrowly specialized in their function. As Khrushchov put it:

We are striving to have our entire youth, millions of boys and girls,
go through the ten-year secondary school. Naturally enough, they
cannot all be absorbed by the colleges . . . In recent years, in view of
the growing numbers passing out of the ten-year schools, a smaller
proportion of boys and girls enter college. The greater part of them . . .
turn out to be quite unprepared for life and do not know in which
direction to turn . . . Owing to the fact that the secondary-school
curriculum is divorced from life, these boys and girls have absolutely
no knowledge of production, and society does not know how best to
utilize these young and vigorous people . . . This state of affairs can
hardly be considered right.[33]

In short, the ten-year schools were trying to give to all an
education specially suited to the needs of a minority. They were
succeeding, it appears, only too well; every year, thousands of
young people worked hard at school with their eyes on a university
place, only to find that for most of them the places were not
forthcoming. Their courses, by fitting them specially for academic
work, had unfitted them for anything else. The result was widespread frustration, increased string-pulling by the influential,
more cramming in the schools, and a rise in the delinquency
figures.

The reformed system, with its stress on work-training for all, sought to avoid this by providing an alternative qualification, by playing up the virtues of work and making industrial labour more palatable, and at the same time building up a better-trained labour force. In principle, there was a good deal of sense in this. What passes for 'general education' is usually as vocational a course as any, designed for those whose work will involve academic rather than technical know-how. To educate all children, or even a sizeable proportion of them, according to the needs of the small fraction who will go on to higher education is asking for trouble, as we are finding out in this country as well. One alternative might have been to introduce a highly selective system, perhaps on the German model, whereby children are selected early for different types of secondary school, one of which caters for the few going on to further academic study. Such a solution, however, would have run completely counter to Soviet educational ideals, and would certainly have given rise to other problems, probably much more serious. The combination of academic and labour training for all seemed a reasonable way out of the difficulty, and had the further advantage of re-defining 'general education' as the education of the citizen and the worker as well as the scholar.

But the reforms attempted rather more. There has been ample evidence since the war that a 'new class' or 'technocracy' has been emerging in the Soviet Union. In spite of periodic attacks on nepotism and 'incorrect social attitudes', most parents in white-collar jobs have done their best to keep their children clear of manual work by pushing them through the schools in the direction of college diplomas and white collars of their own, the whiter the better. Nor has this been confined to the growing élite; many working parents have similar ambitions for their own children, and exert pressure to work hard in school to lift themselves up the social ladder by winning qualifications for some kind of intellectual, or at least non-manual, work. This, of course, is a familiar enough phenomenon in our own country, where the maintaining or improving of social position seems to be the strongest driving-force among parents and pupils alike, for all the lip-service paid to broader educational aims. Many in

Britain condemn this 'rat-race' on a variety of grounds, feeling that we have got our values wrong when so much effort is spent scaling the rungs of social prestige. In the U.S.S.R. the objection is more serious; the latter is not supposed to exist at all, and social climbing is seen as a barrier to the building of the classless society. Khrushchov had a good deal to say about this too:

> We still have a sharp distinction drawn between mental and manual work . . . This is fundamentally wrong and runs counter to our teachings and aspirations. As a rule, boys and girls who have finished secondary school consider that the only acceptable path in life for them is to continue their education at higher schools . . . Some of them even consider [work] beneath their dignity. This scornful and lordly attitude is to be found also in some families. If a boy or girl does not study well . . . and fails to get into college, the parents . . . frighten him by saying that . . . . he will have to work in a factory as a common labourer. Physical work becomes a thing to frighten children with . . . Such views are an insult to the working people of socialist society.
>
> Such an incorrect situation . . . can no longer be tolerated. In socialist society work must be valued by its usefulness, must be stimulated not only by its remuneration, but also by the high respect of our Soviet public. It must be constantly inculcated in the young people that . . . work is a vital necessity for every Soviet person.[34]

The basic motive, then, would seem to have been ideological. As well as oiling the wheels of Soviet society by removing some of the causes of frustration among school-leavers and training the much-needed manpower for the national economy, this was an attempt to teach the dignity of labour, to break down the barriers between mental and manual work, and to check the emergence of a 'new class' in Soviet society. From this point of view, Khrushchov was using an educational reform as a tool for an ambitious piece of social engineering.

Like so many of Khrushchov's schemes, it turned out to be over-ambitious. It is perhaps still too early to be certain about the *long-term* effects of the 'polytechnization' of the schools on social attitudes generally and attitudes to manual work in particular, but so far there is plenty of evidence that the 'white-collar' mentality continues to flourish.[35] It has also been clear for a long time now that whatever benefits might be expected from the linking of technical and mental work in the schools, the wholesale adoption of production training in factories was not having the desired results. Soon after the new law was put into effect, complaints in the Press began to appear; teachers and pupils complained of repetitive and pointless work in the factories, while factory managers were all too often at a complete loss what to do with all the extra hands suddenly put at their disposal. Showing children round factories was one thing, but having hundreds of them under their feet two days a week was quite another. The point was also made, with increasing force, that while some acquaintance with practical work was no doubt a good thing for the pupils' developing attitudes, increasing the length of time spent at it did not necessarily increase its educational value – quite the contrary. Others complained that what the children were in fact doing was not so much general technical training as, all too often, rather ineffective training in jobs they had not the slightest intention of following. The assault on Khrushchov's blanket solution to a real problem went on, until in 1964 the Plenum of the Communist Party recognized that 'in production training serious deficiencies have not yet been overcome, and accordingly it has appeared a complete waste of time.'[36] It was strongly argued, however, that these were deficiencies of organization, not principle:

The chief reasons for such a phenomenon lie in the fact that the necessary procedure has not been introduced everywhere ... There has also been a lack of clarity in the planning of production training ... Many programmes were needlessly overloaded with material not clearly needed ... which artificially prolonged production training and, consequently, the length of course in the secondary school. All this caused serious discontent among pupils and parents, and teachers as well.[37]

Accordingly, in August 1964, the authorities cut back the programme. The decree 'On Changing the Period of Instruction in Secondary General Labour Polytechnical Schools with Production Training' was passed, in which the Council of Ministers charged the relevant ministries with the reorganization and

rationalization of production training. The extra year was removed, the new programmes reduced the total time for polytechnical and production training to a quarter of the total time,
and the changes were phased in within two years.[38]

The removal of the extra year was generally presented as the
result of time-saving by rationalizing existing curricula,[39] but had
probably more to do with overstraining of resources brought
about by the 1958 changes – which, indeed, had still not been
fully implemented in some of the remoter areas. It was em-
phasized, however, that the 1964 measures were not to be taken
as a retreat from the polytechnical principle and all that it im-
plied:

> Education in and for work has become the sacred watch-word of the
> Soviet school . . . This change in no way means a return to the old
> ten-year school, a repudiation of production training. Every teacher,
> every worker in public education must realize, and persistently explain
> to the pupils and the people that the new ten-year school is a labour
> school, a polytechnical school, providing production training for its
> pupils.[40]

This, of course, was not the end of the matter. The 1964 programmes were declared at the time to be transitional; in the
meantime, the ministries and the Academy of Pedagogic Sciences
got to work on a more permanent scheme of things, which was
brought into effect within a couple of years; with some modifications since, it is still in operation.[41] The emphasis has certainly
moved more towards general education, so much so that in 1966,
when the Soviet Minister of Education was elaborating on the
implications of the decision to aim for universal complete secondary education, he described going on to the ninth form as the
best way of continuing one's schooling, rather than going to a
secondary specialized or vocational technical school. Universal
training in production was also dropped. Thus far, many of
Khrushchov's innovations had been abandoned. But much is still
made of the need to 'strengthen the links of the school with
life'.[42] Only exceptionally will this mean the pupils doing productive work in factories – this will be limited to schools where

really suitable facilities exist. But polytechnical education and general work-training are to remain an important element of the curriculum for all pupils. Many Western commentators have been quick to conclude that the events of the last two or three years have marked a complete rejection of the principle of linking general education with practical work, but this seems a rather hasty conclusion. What has happened so far has not been a rejection of the principle, but a reappraisal of the best ways of putting it into practice. How successful this is will take rather longer to emerge. As we have seen, the Basic Law of 1973 confirmed it as a central feature of the educational system, and there has been some strengthening of the practical side. But there still seems to be some uncertainty about the best ways of putting the principle into practice. The present system, whereby pupils do five days of production practice in the fifth, sixth, and seventh classes, and twenty-two in the ninth, seems to be a compromise between the large proportion introduced by Khrushchov in 1958 and its virtual abandonment in most schools only a few years later in 1966. In detail at least, the matter is not closed yet.

Teaching Methods

Like virtually everything else in Soviet education, classroom organization and teaching methods are prescribed by the central authorities. Curricula are, as we have seen, almost uniform throughout the country; not only does the Soviet teacher have to work to a set scheme, but he has to go through a stipulated amount of subject-matter every term, month, and week, and must keep to the approved methods of putting it across to his pupils. 'Correct' teaching techniques are therefore taught in the teacher training institutions, and are enforced in the school by ministerial regulation, by the school director (who is expected to hear the teaching of every member of his staff regularly), and by inspectors from the Departments of Education. This situation is common enough in many Continental countries, East and West, but leaves many British and most American observers aghast at its rigidity.

The prescribed techniques are still, for the most part, formal and old-fashioned, and although attempts are now being made to bring them up to date, teaching methods have been slow to change in the Soviet Union. In the heady atmosphere of experiment in the years after the revolution, the schools tried every 'progressive' technique available, including many importations from the West, such as the Dalton Plan, whereby pupils worked on individual assignments geared to their own pace, or activity methods such as the 'project' inspired by John Dewey; but all this came to an end in the 1930s, when the Stalin régime reintroduced the formal schooling of pre-revolutionary times. The death of Stalin set in motion many changes in various fields of Soviet life, but the classroom was not one of them. Standard Soviet practice still bears a close resemblance to that of the more traditional teachers in this country.

Basically, the lesson is a one-way process; the job of the teacher is to tell the pupils, theirs to accept and absorb. Lesson techniques are therefore closely akin to lecturing, with questioning of the class to make sure that the prescribed material is going home. There is not much place for learning by doing – the role of the children is mainly passive.

The teacher usually begins the lesson by examining the children's homework. This consists largely of the recitation of memorized material, problems solved, sentences translated, etc., or the answering of the teacher's questions by selected pupils, who stand out at the blackboard to say their piece or perform the task required. On average, this kind of thing takes up to twenty per cent of the time. Pupils are given marks for their performances, ranging from five at the top to one at the bottom of the scale; all of them are supposed to be examined thus at regular intervals, and the resultant marks accompany them all the way through the school. This stage of the lesson can be used as a general review of the subject-matter to date, so that the children can all have a clear picture of what has been covered so far.

The next stage is the introduction of new material. Most of this is straight lecturing by the teacher; the children sit and listen attentively while it is explained to them. When he has finished the exposition of the day's lesson, the teacher then questions various members of the class to see if they have understood, and any child in difficulties can take this chance of asking for further explanation. Finally, the children are given their next homework assignment – material from the textbook to learn, or written work – and the teacher summarizes the day's lesson, integrating what is new with what has gone before. Each lesson is thus meant to be a well-defined unit, comprising revision and testing of old material, introduction and elaboration of the new, questioning to see if the point has been grasped, and the setting of homework to reinforce. In practice, it is not always as rigid as this, but such a framework, and the necessity of getting through a set amount of work with a class of mixed ability, leaves little room for spontaneity, activity, or discussion.

The atmosphere of the lesson is as formal as its structure. The children are arranged in rows of desks facing the teacher, in the traditional manner. In accordance with the nationwide 'Rules for Pupils' (see pp. 56–7), they rise when he enters or leaves the room, stand to attention when answering or asking questions or reciting homework, sit up straight with arms folded when listening to the lesson, hold up their hands for permission to speak, sit down only by permission, and so forth. The teacher is in complete control throughout, the children being forbidden by the rules to speak or do anything except with his direction or consent.

This sounds formidable, but is usually far less fearsome in practice. Rigid though the rules sound, there is a good deal of room for interpretation in their application. There are teachers who stick to the prescribed pattern with minute, mechanical precision, and insist on a completely literal interpretation of th rules, reprimanding children (at some length) for holding up their hands in the wrong way, making much of the importance of the proper method of folding the arms, and so on, with all the understanding and imagination of a regular drill-sergeant. On the other hand, many teachers, though keeping within the regulation framework, are much more liberal in their approach; formality is tempered by friendliness. (It is worth noting that this, as well as the maintenance of order, is officially encouraged.) It is quite usual for lessons to be run in the prescribed manner without any feeling of parade-ground tension. Children are expected to stand when addressing the teacher, but not in an automatic jack-in-the-box manner, while the teacher, though still firmly in charge of the class, is careful to show the children the same courtesy he expects of them, using such terms as 'Please', 'Thank you', and so forth to modify the bare command. Teacher–pupil relations seem, on the whole, to be orderly but unstrained. Children do not address the teachers by any formal titles, but use the first name and patronymic;[43] teachers use the first names alone. Incidentally, the existence in Russian of familiar and polite forms of 'you' introduces a complication shared by other European languages but mercifully absent in English. Children in the earlier forms are called by the familiar *ty* (French *tu*), but the polite *vy* (*vous*) is used with the older ones. The Soviet classroom may be rigidly organized by some Western standards (this at any rate is the reaction of most Americans and some Englishmen, though to a Scot the régime is far from unfamiliar); but it is not as soulless and mechanical as a reading of the regulations might suggest.

Recently, there has been considerable movement away from the prevailing verbal formality of lessons. It is now widely recognized that a child learns better what he does than what he hears, and that 'chalk and talk' is a teaching device of limited efficiency. There has been an increase in experiments on teaching method in the pedagogic institutes and the Academy of Pedagogic Sciences, greater emphasis on the use of films, tapes, television, and audio-visual aids of all kinds, while greater attempts are made, through in-service courses for teachers and methods circles in the schools, to acquaint teachers with their use. Partly as a result of experience gained in experiments in polytechnical training, the importance of practical work in the science laboratories is more fully realized. In foreign language teaching, the stress has shifted from formal analysis to mastery of the spoken idiom, and language classes are now supposed to consist of groups of ten to twenty pupils each, not thirty to forty as previously; language laboratories are coming into their own, subject to the availability of the costly equipment required. Programmed learning (the use of so-called 'teaching machines') is experimental but increasing, so much so that worried voices are now heard, complaining that Soviet educationists are in danger of adopting American and other Western techniques in this field too uncritically.[44] It is significant, too, that the new schemes now being introduced for the ten-year school envisage some reduction of formal teaching time, and increased emphasis on independent work by the pupils.

Such developments are important, but should not be exaggerated. Although it is true that modern methods are in much greater use in Soviet schools than they were even five years ago, there are powerful forces for conservatism in teaching. For one thing, they tend to be expensive, requiring as they do considerable investment in equipment; for another, traditional attitudes die hard in the Soviet Union as elsewhere. Altogether, it is much easier to establish English teaching by language laboratories or programmed courses of physics in a school near the centre of things in Moscow or Minsk than in an eight-year school in the rural Ukraine or Kirgizia. For all the advances, traditional classroom teaching retains a powerful hold on the average Soviet school.

Further, teachers still have to stick to the prescribed programme, which leaves little room for discussion, spontaneous inquiry, or for the useful device of letting a digression go its own way. An imaginative teacher can thus be frustrated, or an unimaginative one misled into an obsession with unimportant detail and a preoccupation with outward form. Change is always possible, of course; a teacher with a good idea can refer it to a pedagogic institute or some similar body for research, and it may well be embodied in standard practice. But he is not free to try anything out on his own class on his own initiative, and official channels are liable to become silted up. Also, what might prove a good method for one man or one class might not be a good general rule for teaching, a point which educational officials are slow to appreciate.

But it is unlikely that the run-of-the-mill teacher sees things in this light. Most teachers in most countries rely heavily on copying normal practice for the basis of their own teaching. Where they are left free to decide entirely on their own methods, many either follow closely in their senior colleagues' ways, or flounder helplessly in the absence of any clear indication of what they should do; where methods are substantially prescribed, as in the Soviet schools, they can use as a prop what others regard as a hindrance. It should be remembered, too, that there are still many Soviet teachers whose training has been limited to secondary pedagogic schools (see pp. 152–3). The system has at least the merit of making reasonably competent teachers out of people who would not achieve anything like their present successes if left to their own devices.

Central control of teaching methods, then, combines security for the mediocre or shaky teacher with restriction for the lively and adventurous; and for all the recent emphasis on the improvement of techniques, abdication of this control and its devolution to the class teacher remains highly unlikely. The frequent dullness of the formal lesson is more likely to go, though this will take some time; meanwhile, it is just as well that the teacher can rely to a considerable extent on the widespread national reverence for education, and the individual child's eagerness to learn.

5. Higher Education

The Growth of Higher Education

Of all the advances in the educational field since the revolution, few have provided more cause for pride on the part of the Soviet authorities and anxiety for some Western observers than the spread of higher education in the universities and other institutions. The figures of growth are certainly eloquent: in 1914 there were 105 institutions, including eight universities, most of them concentrated in the major cities of European Russia; by 1959 there were 766 institutions, forty of them universities, spread over the entire country. There were 127,400 students of all kinds in 1914, 2,150,000 in 1959; 10,700 graduated in 1914, 342,200 in 1959. The numbers of men and women in higher education are roughly equal. The numbers continue to rise;[1] 403,900 graduated in 1965, and by 1965–6 the total number of students had risen to 3,861,000.[2] By the end of the decade, over half a million were graduating every year, and the number of students had passed the $4\frac{1}{2}$ million mark. By 1976, there were over three-quarters of a million graduates a year, and a total enrolment of nearly five million. In the early days of the Soviet régime, the problem was to find enough trained graduates for the public need; now it is to find some way of coping with the rising tide of would-be entrants for whom the institutions have no places – one of the considerations, as we have seen, behind the 1958 reforms.

Not only has there been a spectacular rise in the number of higher educational places, but their distribution among the various peoples of the U.S.S.R. has been made more equable.

Tadzhikistan, for example, which before 1917, had no facilities for higher education and few for any other kind, now has thirty-three special and technical schools, eight institutions of higher education, and an Academy of Sciences. In 1917 the more backward areas generally (Siberia, Central Asia, the Far East) had four institutions; now, with over 200, they account for about a quarter of the country's output of graduates. In some of the Union Republics, such as Georgia, Armenia, and Uzbekistan, it is possible to take a full higher educational course in the native language. This is not the case everywhere, however, and there are signs that in many areas Russian is expanding at the expense of the local tongue, especially where the minorities are small, the local cultures less firmly rooted, and the proportion of Russian-speaking settlers high. This is particularly true of areas like Kazakhstan, where the last two of these conditions apply. But where the indigenous culture is well established, even small republics like Armenia make extensive use of the vernacular. The University of Yerevan, for example, admits a number of students from Third World countries, as do many higher institutes in the U.S.S.R. Like them, it requires the students to take a preliminary year for language study; but in this case, the language is Armenian, not Russian. Erevan is not by any means unique in this respect, though rather more determined than most.

A large proportion of Soviet students consists of working people who study in their spare time. For what can still be considered a poor country, compared with the U.S.A. or Western Europe, the financial burden of higher education on the national economy is immense. One method of keeping costs down has been to save on the standard of students' hostel accommodation, which makes it possible for the Soviet authorities to consider the very ordinary students' rooms in Moscow University as something of a showpiece. Another has been to encourage various types of part-time education. This has obvious financial attractions, and has at times been presented (especially during the Khrushchov period) as ideologically desirable as well, a means of fighting academic exclusiveness by keeping as many students as possible close to the realities of working life. More important still, the fact that part-time students stay at their jobs ensures that the expansion of higher education does not mean too great a drain on the labour force. Correspondence students are not, however, left to their own devices till they sit their examinations; they are expected to visit the institution to which they are attached for periodic consultation with tutors, short courses of lectures and seminars, leave from work being readily granted for the purpose.[3] In this way it has been possible to reduce the casualty rate of students who find the pressure of work too much and give up before completing their courses. The success rate is higher than it used to be, but the courses for part-time students are still a very heavy burden on top of their normal work, and often take longer as a result. This has given rise to some controversy. After the Khrushchov reforms, it seemed certain that part-time higher education would be the main growth-point. For a time, it was; by 1959, part-time students accounted for forty-five per cent of the total (thirty-eight per cent correspondence, seven per cent evening and shift students). The 1950s saw a spectacular growth of part-time facilities, correspondence courses being more than doubled and evening-class places multiplying ninefold, while full-time places grew more modestly. By 1965, over half of all students were part-timers, 1,708,000 correspondence and 569,000 evening students, compared with 1,584,000 in full-time study. But as the part-time places increased, so did the complaints. Doubts were raised about the quality of many of the courses, and there was concern about the much higher drop-out rate – according to one study,[4] nearly double that in full-time courses. Also, the effects of the Second World War on the labour force had become less pressing with the passage of time, so that one of the arguments for the emphasis on part-time study lost some of its weight. Consequently, arrangements for part-time courses have been tightened up – preference is given, for example, to applicants for courses which are relevant to their work – and the proportion of part-timers is falling once again. It was still over half in 1969–70, with 1,742,000 correspondence and 668,000 evening students as against 2,140,000 full-time, but this was a drop from the previous year. This trend has continued. Since 1968, over half the *entrants* have been full-time students, an indication of the way things were going. By 1977, there were 2,711,000 full-time students, compared with 650,000 in evening classes and 1,589,000 studying by correspondence. The part-time system, it seems, is proving rather expensive in some ways, and is likely to play a less prominent role in the future. But it still has a part to play in raising the number of available graduates, and providing opportunities for higher education for many individuals who, in an entirely full-time system, would almost certainly have had to do without.

The Aims of Higher Education

Institutions of higher education, like every other branch of the system, are organized with the social, political, and economic needs of Soviet society continually in mind. The objectives of higher education, as well as its structure and organization, are defined by law in the 'Statute on the Higher Schools of the U.S.S.R.', approved by the Council of Ministers in 1961 and assimilated into the Basic Law of 1973. This law lays down the aims of the universities and colleges as follows:

1. To train highly qualified specialists educated in the spirit of Marxism–Leninism, well-versed in both the latest achievements of science and technology, at home and abroad, and in the practical aspects of production, capable of utilizing modern technology to the utmost and of creating the technology of the future.
2. To carry out research that will contribute to the solution of the problems of building communism.
3. To produce textbooks and study aids of a high standard.
4. To train teachers and research workers.
5. To provide advanced training for specialists with higher education working in various fields of the national economy, the arts, education, and the health services.
6. To disseminate scientific and political knowledge among the people.
7. To study the problems connected with the utilization of graduates and with improving the quality of their training.[5]

Much of this sounds more like rhetoric than a programme for action, but statements of this kind serve to show that the authorities do not regard the functions of higher educational establishments as limiting to teaching. The emphasis on research is new, as is the stress on the importance of close cooperation with the various branches of the national economy. It is held to be essential to maintain this close relationship; a great deal of current scientific and industrial research is carried on as a joint enterprise under the aegis of industrial managements and higher educational bodies. Although most institutes come under the jurisdiction of the Ministry of Higher Education, some of the more specialized are run by other ministries, notably those of Health and Culture, and closely integrated with their general plans for development and research. The role of higher education as a producer of knowledge as well as a teaching process is given more attention as time goes on.

The expected stress on political work, training specialists 'educated in the spirit of Marxism–Leninism', and spreading 'scientific and political knowledge among the people', shows how far the authorities regard graduates as a vanguard in the construction of the new society. It is their job not only to exercise their specialist skills, but also to understand, accept, and propagate the political ideas of the régime, so that they can act as leaders in the various tasks required by the needs of developing Soviet society, as interpreted by the Communist Party. This results in much attention being given to the student's 'social' as well as academic record – he is expected to spend some of his holiday and spare time on voluntary work for the community, such as helping to build the underground railway in Leningrad, or helping with the harvest in nearby agricultural areas. This emphasis on the student's political role also results in the lengthy and detailed (and compulsory) courses in Marxist–Leninist political theory for all students, regardless of their speciality or future job.

The Structure of Higher Education

Soviet institutions of higher education, like the courses offered in them, are on the whole more specialized than their British counterparts. A course in geology, electrical engineering, or industrial chemistry is usually more limited than would be the case here. Only in the universities is there anything approaching a liberal arts course, but even there the range of studies is narrower, if sometimes deeper; there is no equivalent to Scottish Ordinary or English General Degree, nor do they start on a wide general course, and specialize later, as some of our universities do. Students have to choose their field of study when they apply for admission to an institution. Changes, of course, are possible, but infrequent, as this means taking longer to qualify; as most courses last five years, few students feel inclined to take longer than they can help.

The institutions themselves are more specialized than ours, a clear division normally being drawn between the humanities and pure sciences on the one hand, which are taught at the universities, and practical and applied studies on the other, which are taught at institutes of other types. Many disciplines which we are accustomed to dealing with in university faculties, such as law, medicine, engineering, agriculture, and the like, are studied in separate establishments[6] such as Law Colleges and Medical Institutes. In theory at least the universities and other colleges reach the same standard and enjoy the same status and esteem; in practice, perhaps inevitably, there are some inequalities between the universities and the rest in terms of prestige at least, partly because of their broader curriculum and partly because of the traditional respect for the universities, which dates from pre-revolutionary days. There is, however, no clear-cut official differentiation of status, such as exists in some other countries; some institutes, in fact, such as the Kalinin Polytechnical Institute in Leningrad, enjoy a much higher esteem than many of the universities. All institutions, university and other, have the power of conferring diplomas, conducting research, and awarding post-graduate degrees. The word VUZ (*Vysshee Uchebnoe*

Zavedenie, Higher Educational Institution) is popularly used to refer to all types.

In accordance both with the needs of the national economy and the importance laid by Marxism on the unity of theory and practice, the weight of numbers is strongly in favour of the practical and applied studies. Soviet sources give the broad categories of students in higher education thus: industry and construction, 40·1 per cent; transport and communications, 5·8 per cent; agriculture, 9·6 per cent; economics and law, 7·3 per cent; medicine, physical education, and sport, 7·8 per cent; art and film, 1·0 per cent; and education 29·1 per cent. (Figures rounded off.) This last category applies principally to teacher training, but also includes for convenience most university students in the humanities and the pure sciences alike. However crude the classification, the strength of the technological bias is obvious.

The main types of VUZ are as follows:

Universities

There are sixty-five universities in the U.S.S.R., at least one in each constituent republic, with a total of 580,000 students. A few, like those of Moscow and Leningrad, have a long history by Russian standards, stretching back into the eighteenth and early nineteenth centuries respectively. Others, like the University of Novosibirsk, are of much more recent creation. They vary greatly in size and amenities; Moscow University has over 32,000 students and a staff of 3,700, compared with total enrolments of a thousand or less in some of the new foundations; its science faculties are housed in a massive thirty-two storey building on the Lenin Hills, containing, among other things, 148 lecture halls, over 1,000 laboratories, 6,000 living-rooms, lounges, workrooms, and a library with over 5,000,000 titles. The building was completed in 1953. Leningrad University's premises, by way of contrast, are old and even seedy; new buildings are being planned, a move welcomed by a staff hard-pressed for space. (Some students and teachers, however, have a sentimental regard for the old buildings. One student remarked that he preferred them to the heavy vulgarity of the Moscow skyscraper, which he described as 'new, without being modern'.) Moscow is certainly untypical in many ways; Soviet universities have much the same range as British ones in size, facilities, and state of repair, if not in age.

Broadly, their function is to provide facilities for study and research in the pure sciences and the humanities. The range of available subjects varies a good deal from place to place, but most of them have faculties of physical sciences, mathematics, biology, chemistry, geology, geography, history, philology, and similar familiar disciplines. Some of them have faculties or departments for studies more commonly catered for in separate institutes. There are departments of law, for example, in the Universities of Moscow, Leningrad, Yerevan, and Tbilisi; of economics in Moscow, Leningrad, Kazakhstan, and Tomsk; of journalism in Moscow, Lvov, and Azerbaidzhan, and elsewhere. The major Universities of Moscow and Leningrad are, as can be seen, particularly versatile, and include departments of art history and oriental studies which most other universities do not possess. Departments of philology deal not only with literature and linguistics, but offer courses in a wide range of languages; no less than seventy Soviet and foreign languages are taught somewhere in the U.S.S.R., from Russian, English, and German to Kazakh, Greek, and Vietnamese.

For the most part university students are trained with a view to employment as scientists, scholars, linguists, historians, and the like. Many of them, however, go into teaching, either at academic or school level. In order to keep a pool of potential teachers ready to hand, the authorities require most university students to take courses in psychology, educational theory, and teaching methods, and to do a certain amount of teaching practice. (This does not, of course, apply to students whose courses commit them to other professions, such as law.) In this way extra specialist teachers can be recruited when other sources prove insufficient.

Technical Institutes

Over two and a quarter million students are enrolled in technical institutes, of which there are two main types: *polytechnical institutes*, such as those of Leningrad, Kharkov, Kaunas, and the Urals, have between seven and fifteen faculties, offering courses in a variety of technological subjects such as metallurgy, chemical technology, electrical engineering, precision mechanics, and a host of others. *Branch technical institutes* are more specialized; each one is normally restricted to one particular industry, such as the Mining Institute at Dnepropetrovsk, the Moscow Power Institute, or the Civil Engineering Institute at Novosibirsk. The combination of practical work experience and theoretical knowledge is particularly stressed at technical institutes of both types, several continuous periods of work in factories and workshops forming an essential part of the course.

Agricultural Institutes

These colleges are very similar to the technical institutes in principle and function, turning out specialists in various branches of agriculture, such as agronomy, pomology, and gardening, soil chemistry, animal husbandry, veterinary medicine, agricultural economics, the mechanization of agriculture, and so forth. Theoretical studies are combined with periods of practical work on experimental plots and the collective and state farms. While the impact of higher education on agriculture has been noticeably less than on industry, it seems that the fault lies with the organization of farms and farm policy rather than with the colleges or their graduates. Most of the recent complaints have been directed at the misuse of specialists rather than their quality, though some have been taken to task for being too academic in their approach – or, as Khrushchov put it (pungently if rather unfairly), 'They cannot tell young hemp from nettles until they have been stung by the nettles.' This kind of criticism has been common lately in many fields of education, hence the increased stress on the need for practical experience. There are over 414,000 agriculture students in the U.S.S.R.

Medical Institutes

Soviet doctors are trained in the medical institutes, with an enrolment of over 356,000 students. These colleges also provide six-year courses, not for general practitioners, which are not found in Soviet medicine, but for specialists in such fields as internal medicine, pediatrics, sanitation, stomatology, pharmaceutics, etc., and offer refresher courses in which graduates can keep abreast of the latest developments in their own fields. At the present time, three-quarters of practising doctors are women, partly because of the special conditions created by the civil war, the rush to industrialize in the 1920s and 1930s, and the Second World War. The balance is changing, however, and a large minority (forty-three per cent) of Soviet medical students are now men.

In addition to doctors and nurses, Soviet medicine recognizes a second-grade medical practitioner, known as a *feldsher*, somewhere between the two professions in depth of knowledge and extent of responsibility. They are not trained at the medical institutes, however, which provide courses for doctors only; *feldshera*, like nurses, receive their training at the appropriate specialized secondary schools.

Pedagogic Institutes

These are concerned with the training of teachers and will be dealt with in the next chapter.

Institutes of Economics

Twenty-five specialist colleges train the large number of economists needed for the planning and management of the elaborate machinery of the Soviet industrial and agricultural system. Here again, the tendency is to specialize in some particular field – political economy, planning and production accounting, the economics of industry, transport and agriculture, finance, and so forth. Fourteen universities and sixty-one agricultural and technical institutes also train economists, the universities being more concerned with theory and the other establishments with its practical application to their own field. The subject is, of course, presented from the Marxist point of view, but other economic theorists, such as John Maynard Keynes, are introduced in the syllabus so that they can be proved wrong. There are over 609,000 economic students.

Law Institutes

There are over 95,000 law students in the U.S.S.R. Their studies include a broad common course of legal subjects ranging from Theory of Law and State and Roman Law to Accounting and Forensic Medicine, together with a choice of three special fields: State and Administrative Law (including fundamentals of national economic planning, history of the Soviet state and law, administration, etc.); Criminal Law (including criminology, criminal action, appeals, court organization); and Civil Law, including land, collective-farm, labour, patent, planning, and contract law, etc. Courses in these various branches are provided at the special law institutes, and also in the new faculties and departments of some universities. Here too theoretical learning is combined with practical training, which takes the form of work in government offices and selected branches of the legal service, the nearest equivalent to the kind of legal apprenticeship known in this country.

Arts Institutes

This category covers a variety of establishments, most of which concentrate on one aspect of the fine or applied arts. It includes twenty-three music conservatories, nine institutes of drama and scenic design, ten academies and institutes of the visual and plastic arts, as well as institutes of decorative and applied arts, industrial art schools, a literary institute, three architectural institutes, and a college of cinematography. Entry to these is in theory open to all comers who can satisfy the entrance requirements, but in practice those who have been to the special schools for the gifted in the arts get the bulk of the places in most of them, especially in the music conservatories. Courses are a combination of practical work and study of theory, but here the emphasis is overwhelmingly on the production of competent practitioners in the visual arts, music, drama, and the like. There are over 45,000 students in courses of this type. A number of universities also provide courses for those more interested in the theoretical or historical side.

Institutes of Physical Culture
There are sixteen Institutes of Physical Culture. Their function is to train instructors in physical education, gymnastics, and sport.

Admission and Maintenance of Students

Competition for entry to Soviet higher education is keen, even fierce. All Soviet citizens under the age of thirty-five who have successfully completed a full secondary-school course and obtained the 'Certificate of Maturity' (*Attestat zrelosti*) are eligible to apply for admission, but in practice there is room in the institutions for only a fraction of these. The proportion of applicants accepted varies from place to place, ranging from one in three to one in eight. In some extreme cases the pressure is even greater: the Leningrad Mechanics and Optics Institute, for example, admitted only one applicant in thirty in 1958. In recent years, the number of available places has risen somewhat, while the number of aspiring entrants has rocketed. For this reason, the automatic admission of gold medallists from the secondary schools has been dropped, although they are still at an advantage, all other things being equal; entry is now determined by the would-be student's performance in competitive examination, and by his place on the list of priorities.

The exact form of the entry examination depends on the faculty or speciality that the student has in mind. Russian language and literature, a foreign language, and the language of the republic (in the case of non-Russian institutions) are general requirements. In addition, students must satisfy the examiners of their competence in their proposed fields of study – physics, chemistry, and mathematics for intending scientists and engineers, history and geography for intending lawyers and students of the humanities, and art and music for those trying to enter the art academies and music conservatories, and so forth. This requirement is intended to put a stop to the growing practice whereby some students entered courses not because of interest but simply because they were easier to get into; many of them would switch over to their real interest when a place became available. This was condemned on a number of grounds, such as waste of time, parasitism, and so forth, and because more genuine applicants were kept out.

The examinations are partly written, partly oral, and are assessed on the usual five-point scale, from five (excellent) to one (poor), thus making a total possible score of twenty-five. Normally a total of twenty-three is needed, though 'mature' students – ex-servicemen and ex-workers – may be let in with twenty-one. This procedure is uniform throughout the country, but the actual standard is not, since each institution is largely responsible for running its own examinations, with some supervision from the Ministry. Accordingly, there are some discrepancies in standards: they are higher for polytechnical institutes than for agricultural colleges, for example, and higher for universities than for pedagogic institutes, in spite of the theoretical equality of status. Even among institutes of the same kind there are some variations; university entrance is difficult anywhere, but much more so in Moscow or Leningrad than in Alma-Ata or Dushanbe. This results in some heart-burning among unsuccessful applicants who have miscalculated their chances. As one disappointed youth put it, 'I wasn't clever enough to get into Leningrad, just enough to make it seem worth trying. That's what makes it so hard.'

There are other considerations too. Preference is given, other things being equal, to students who can produce a reference (*kharakteristika*) from Party or Komsomol organizations, trade unions, or their factory managers, and to those who have served in the armed forces. In Khrushchov's day, strong preference was also given to *stazhniki*, people who had worked for at least two years after leaving school. By the early 1960s, the proportion of *stazhniki* was running at about eighty per cent; the remaining twenty per cent who came straight from school were mostly mathematicians or physicists, on the grounds that their special skills were likely to come early to fruition (and also, no doubt, because they were in short supply).

Students' opinions of this requirement were mixed. Some felt it did them good, like the Moscow students who told a visitor: 'We know ourselves better and we are more enthusiastic about what we want to do after working with others on the farms and in the factories.' Others regarded it as a monumental waste of time, like the young man in Leningrad who was trying to get into the Faculty of Geography in the university after working for two years on building sites: 'Carrying bricks is a poor preparation for getting through the entrance exams, and I've forgotten a lot of my school work. If I fail this time I'll try again, certainly, but by next year I'll have forgotten still more.' Others again were in favour of 'seeing something of life first' in principle, but were unenthusiastic about its application to themselves in particular.

Not only was the insistence on the two-year *stazh* of work experience unpopular with most students, it was also doubtfully effective, either educationally or socially. According to the study already mentioned, *stazhniki* experienced a good deal of difficulty in getting back into the habit of studying, and were particularly liable to drop out. While about a quarter of those coming straight from school failed to finish, the figure for the *stazhniki* was over forty-five per cent. Nor had this policy done as much as had been expected to equalize the educational opportunities of various social groups. In spite of a variety of 'loading' devices, the children of professional people ('specialists') still have a better chance than anyone else of entering higher education. Actually, the most serious gap is not between the specialists and the rest, but between urban and rural children. One recent survey [7] showed that, in the region under examination, eighty-two per cent of 'specialists'' children who had finished the ten-year school went on to some kind of further education; the proportion for urban workers' children was sixty-one per cent, but for the children of peasants it was only ten per cent. Simply loading the entrance groups with class quotas has not proved, in itself, enough to remedy this, since students from the country areas form yet another group particularly liable to drop out. Present policy tends to make less of work-requirements and quotas, and more of practical help, such as the 'preparatory years' recently initiated in a number of universities and colleges.

Once admitted, students in higher education receive all tuition free of charge; the only fees payable are hostel charges, which are little more than nominal, for those not living at home. Apart from the few (between ten and twenty per cent) whose parents' incomes are too high to qualify them for government aid, students who maintain satisfactory progress are awarded stipends. These can be forfeited if the quality of work falls off. Students to whom this happens (and there do not seem to be many of them) are allowed to continue their studies, but receive no state help until their work improves. They can be expelled altogether if this improvement is not forthcoming.

Students' stipends in higher educational institutions now vary around half the average working wage, depending on their special field and a year of study. These are the amounts for satisfactory students; those with consistently good performances can gain an additional fifteen to twenty per cent, according to their examination marks. Higher stipends are paid in some fields, such as mechanical as opposed to chemical engineering, or science as opposed to medicine, in order to attract a higher number of better applicants. This varies in accordance with the state requirements from time to time. There are also 'personal stipends' (*personal'nye imennye stipendii*), commemorative scholarships paid in addition to the basic stipends; these are awarded only to really outstanding students.

Soviet official pronouncements make much of the system of student stipends, which certainly presents a marked contrast to conditions in pre-revolutionary times. Actually they are far from enough; the average student's stipend is insufficient for even the barest necessities, and it seems to be accepted, at least in the major cities, that the family, or work, must supplement it. Many students have to rely on help from their families to make ends meet, and some manage to make extra money by taking part-time jobs, such as scene-shifting in theatres or as extras in film-studios, as well as more common and less glamorous casual work. They are expected to join their trade union, and practically all do so. This costs two per cent of the monthly stipend, but carries economic advantages, such as subsidized holidays at student health resorts, reduced prices at theatres, cinemas, and concert halls, and other concessions of this kind. There is a general feeling that student stipends are quite inadequate; but while the economy is as heavily burdened as at present, there is not likely to be any spectacular improvement. Students at Moscow University who complained about their grants were told by Khrushchov that the subsistence level in the U.S.S.R. was reckoned at twenty-five roubles a month, and most of them were doing a good deal better than that. Stipends have risen since then, as of course have costs (and, it should be added, so have expectations); in relative terms, it can hardly be called a dramatic improvement. Other aspects of the educational system stand much higher on the priority list as long as students can just get by.

Courses, Curricula, and Assignment of Graduates

Courses in most institutions of higher education last for five years, though some, such as specialist medicine, geology, some branches of technology and engineering, and part-time courses, are a year or so longer. Each year is divided into two terms (*semestry*), from September to January and from February to June, with vacations of two weeks in the winter and two months in the summer – a long academic year by Western standards. Furthermore, the student's time is packed during term. Instruction can extend to as much as six hours a day, six days a week, consisting of formal lectures, seminars, laboratory work, and practical studies, to say nothing of the enormous amount of reading required during the rest of the time. Some weeks each year are set aside for examinations, preparation of dissertations, and the like, so that formal instruction does not fill more than about thirty or so weeks in the year. Nevertheless, with a total of over five thousand hours of teaching spread over the five years (not counting extra optional subjects), the student's time actually under instruction is roughly twice as great as that of his Western counterpart. Since continued progress is a condition of the payment of stipends and even of continued attendance, there is little room for the leisurely academic or the dilettante. All lectures and seminars are compulsory, though 'cutting' of classes is not unknown. Prescribed reading lists in some departments are so lengthy that for even the most conscientious student it is physically impossible to get through them all – hence much reliance, as the examinations draw near, on the time-honoured international practice of 'spotting' likely questions in advance.

The overloading of students' time is defended by some officials and academics on the grounds that plenty of good hard work is somehow laudable for its own sake, but there is a growing feeling that it has gone too far. At a conference[8] of teachers in higher education as long ago as 1961, many speakers voiced their disquiet about the effects of this mass of lectures, seminars, and prescribed reading, not only because of the strain but because it left too little time for independent work, and put too great a premium on mechanical learning and regurgitation. For example, Academician I. N. Vekua, Rector of Novosibirsk University, had no doubts about the lecture system itself, which he described as 'a method proved by time, with many positive features, and fully justified'. But reliance on this system alone, he said, led to 'a passive attitude in the student, whose principal task becomes that of attending lectures, studying notes and swollen textbooks, and taking exams. This is an essential element in learning, but it is bad when it becomes an end in itself.' At another conference on the training of scientists,[9] Dr Blokhintsev, Director of the Joint Nuclear Research Institute and a corresponding member of the Academy of Sciences of the U.S.S.R., made a similar point in terms that call to mind Khrushchov's pungent turn of phrase. Complaining that the schools, by relying on passive learning, equipped the students poorly for independent work, he went on:

The worst feature is that such a youth feels himself a schoolboy at college too. He is expected to read textbooks, pass tests, attend compulsory lectures, and least of all to show independence. He is thus taught so much that he leaves college like a stuffed fish. People may have different ideas about its content, but one thing is certain: it cannot swim.

It seems that some of the authorities at least are aware of the effects of undue reliance on lecture-absorption and textbook-learning, but as yet there are few signs of the students' burdens being appreciably lightened.

All students, whatever their special field, have to attend courses and pass examinations in Marxist–Leninist political theory. These consist of classes in the History of the Communist Party of the Soviet Union (a survey of the history of the U.S.S.R. and twentieth-century world events from the approved political standpoint) during the first two years. Political economy and dialectical and historical materialism make their appearance in the third year, and include a fairly detailed study of Marxist philosophy and economic, political, aesthetic, social, and historical theory. These political courses occupy a considerable part of the students' time; for those studying the humanities, they amount to about 600 hours over the five years. Technologists and scientists, with the greater demands of practical work, have rather less, but even for them Marxist courses take up a total of 300 hours of lectures and exercises. This side of higher education is taken very seriously by the authorities, but according to reports in the Soviet Press is often taught mechanically and dogmatically, with the result that many students regard it as something to be learned for the examinations and then forgotten once the graduation requirements have been fulfilled. In many institutions apathy is so widespread that it is common practice for students to carry on with their other work during the political lectures. How openly they do this depends largely on the quality of the teaching. As one student put it, 'We study for our other subjects only in the back seats if the lecturer is someone who has our respect and interest. If he is not, we work in the front seats as well.' Some claim that they could not get through the required reading in their specialities if they did not do this. (The lists are certainly of daunting length and much of the material monumentally dull. There is a great deal of Marx and Lenin, of course, plus many speeches by Brezhnev, whose style is hardly lively.) Others reportedly sleep through the lectures. In spite of demands for livelier political teaching, many of the tutors apparently feel that there is safety in dullness, since these are potentially thorny subjects; even in the mildest days of the post-Stalin 'thaw', orthodoxy in this field was still considered more important than vividness, and the climate has grown markedly chillier in the last few years. Meanwhile, there are many instances of students, still interested in politics and philosophy but repelled by the aridity of the official courses, running informal 'neo-Marxist' discussion groups among themselves.

As for the students' attitudes to the basic doctrines underlying the political courses, few seem to accept Marxist–Leninist theory in detail as interpreted by the Party, except for those working towards careers in the Party *apparat* through the universities and their Komsomol organs. Few again turn completely from Marxism in favour of something else, such as Christianity, though there are some. For the most part they seem either to accept the broad outlines of Marxism, for want of anything else, or to shrug it off as of little relevance to their own lives, interests, and ambitions, paying little attention to the subject at lectures and less outside. Information on this point is scanty and generalization difficult, but it does appear that making the courses compulsory, in itself, achieves little. This is causing the authorities some concern, since it makes nonsense of the original object of including such courses at all, namely to secure commitment rather than mere conformity. Frequent demands are made for more discussion and less dogmatism in political teaching, though how far this has made any difference is difficult to determine. What many see as the authorities' cavalier way with Marxist principle and even Soviet law (in hounding dissidents, for example) is inclined to reinforce cynicism rather than anything else.

Apart from political studies and other compulsory subjects (a foreign language and physical education), a student's curriculum is confined throughout his course to his special study and a number of allied subjects. These can cover a wide field, rather superficially in some cases but useful enough as aids to the main subject of study. The specialist in Russian language and literature has to profess not only such expected subjects as linguistic theory, literary history, Old Slavonic, etc., but also Latin, a choice of Ukrainian or Byelorussian, and another Slav language; the Spanish or Italian specialist must also study French, Latin, and comparative Romance philology, as well as relevant historical and literary subjects; the historian has to offer Latin, archaeology, ethnology, and a number of specially selected periods, in addition to the fundamental historical studies. All curricula are prescribed by the Republic or U.S.S.R. Ministry of Higher Education, and are generally uniform throughout the country for any particular subject. Certain institutions (generally the more eminent) may draw up their own curricula (*individual'nye plany*), but these have to be accepted by the relevant ministry. At the advanced level there tends to be more variation, but this too is subject to ministerial approval.

Students are assessed continually throughout their courses. This is done by means of essays, laboratory work, homework assignments, tests, and term examinations, usually a combination of written and oral, marked on a four-point scale from distinction to failure. (These also are prescribed in the official syllabus.) The final test is the diploma thesis or, as it is known in the technical institutes, the diploma project. This is a study of some particular aspect of the student's speciality, in which he has to make use of the basic material of his subject and demonstrate his ability to use it for research or experiment. The student is allowed considerable time to prepare his diploma work – the entire second term of the final year in most cases – then presents it at the end of the year, and has to defend it in oral examination before a board which includes professors of the institute and representatives of the ministry. If it is accepted he is awarded his diploma; it is sometimes given with distinction, depending not only on the quality of this one piece of work, but also on his performance at the oral examination and his past academic record.

Graduates can be assigned for two or three years to any job in any part of the Soviet Union; at the end of this time they are free to seek employment wherever they wish. (This does not apply to graduates of part-time courses.) The main reason for this system is that there is no other way of adequately staffing schools, institutions, and industrial enterprises in the remote areas of the U.S.S.R., especially since there is still a marked discrepancy between town and country in living standards and amenities. There is no shortage of skilled manpower in the metropolitan centres such as Moscow, Leningrad, or Kiev – there is even a surplus in some fields – but direction seems to be the only way to get graduates to work in the isolated parts of Siberia and Central Asia, or, for that matter, in any rural area; some would prefer a city in Siberia (Novosibirsk is as big as Glasgow) to a village in the depths of the Leningrad *oblast*. All travelling expenses to the new job are paid by the employer, and graduates who fail to report to their assigned posts are, in theory at least, liable to legal penalties. In practice this never seems to happen, though there is a good deal of dodging by individuals who flatly refuse to spend three years at the back of beyond. The institutions are supposed to send the graduate's diploma to his new employer, so that he forfeits it if he fails to appear, but this does not always happen either; there is an unascertainable but large amount of string-pulling behind the scenes. Certain categories of graduates are awarded a 'free diploma' (*svobodnyi diplom*) which releases them from assignments altogether. The regulations are complicated, but they exempt such people as serving members of the armed forces or graduates with dependent relatives; health considerations are also taken into account; married couples are not separated. Otherwise, on the whole, first choice of the more attractive jobs is given to the better students. As a result, enterprises in the remote areas tend to be staffed by the less outstanding graduates, and often have to put up with a disconcertingly fast turnover of personnel. On the other hand, since good work in unattractive posts is one way of displaying conscientiousness and gaining promotion, they may also have, for a time at least, a few of the more talented and ambitious graduates in their employ to leaven the lump of the more mediocre. Although Soviet students are taught to regard their job assignments as a partial return to society for the benefits of higher education, the system has obvious disadvantages, and there is evidence that the authorities are very greatly concerned at the amount of dodging. Considering the size of the country, and the unevenness of the distribution of population, it is hard to see what else could be done if new areas are to be opened up and the economy to expand. There is also the advantage that graduates are assured of employment in their own field at the end of their course, even if not in the area of their choice; graduate unemployment is unknown in the U.S.S.R.

Higher Degrees and Research

The range of degrees and certificates is more uniform and less complicated in the U.S.S.R. than in Britain, partly because the system is centrally controlled and partly because there is no clearcut distinction between degree-awarding institutions and others. All institutions offer only one qualification for their basic courses – diploma (*diplom*), with or without distinction; there is no differentiation corresponding to our ordinary, general, and honours degrees. At the post-diploma level, two higher degrees can be taken: Candidate of Sciences (*Kandidat nauk*), and Doctor of Sciences (*Doktor nauk*). Both require advanced study and original research, and carry considerable financial advantages and social prestige for their possessors. In spite of their titles, these degrees are not limited to the scientific field any more than our own Ph.D. is limited to the study of philosophy.

The degree of Candidate of Sciences (or of Pedagogic or Technical or Medical Sciences, etc.) requires at least three years of further study after graduation, in accordance with special programmes adopted by the institution and approved by the ministry, with an examination at the end. In addition, the aspiring Candidate (*aspirant*) must conduct a piece of original research for publication in his own field, and defend it at a public hearing before an examining board appointed by the appropriate institution. Few graduates are admitted to higher degree work direct from their diploma course, but usually have to work for two years or more before they can apply. Financial support for full-time post-graduate students is much more generous than for undergraduates, often amounting to as much as their normal salary; many stay in their jobs and study in their spare time. Equivalents can be misleading, but the Soviet Candidate degree is probably somewhere about the standard of a British Ph.D.

The degree of Doctor of Sciences is much more rarely awarded, and is regarded as an extremely high academic distinction. To qualify for this honour, a specialist must hold the Candidate degree, have done several years of active work in his field, and conducted and published major independent research, which he eventually has to defend before an academic council. V. P. Yelyutin, U.S.S.R. Minister of Higher Education, reports that in the twenty years from 1937 to 1957 12,000 Doctorates were awarded in the entire country, compared with over 100,000 Candidate degrees.

Strictly speaking, higher degrees are awarded not by the institution but by the Ministry of Higher Education. The institution makes the recommendation, but confirmation lies with the Ministry's Higher Qualification Commission, known as the V.A.K. (*Vysshaya attestatsionnaya kommissiya*). By all accounts, this confirmation is far from automatic, especially in the case of doctorates. One result of this system is that work for higher degrees can be done outside the higher educational institutions altogether. Out of nearly 26,000 *aspiranty* graduating in 1969, over 10,000 had been studying in higher research institutes, which are quite separate. There are nearly 100,000 post-graduate students, 57,000 of whom are studying in VUZy, which still leaves research institutes with a substantial role in the higher degree system.

Until recently, all members of the teaching staffs of institutions of higher education were required to spend an average of three hours a day on research. Such precision seems to have proved impracticable, and it is now stated that there is more flexibility in the allocation of time between research and teaching.

But research is still regarded as supremely important, and an integral part of the work of higher institutions, both because it is vital to the interests of Soviet society and because it keeps the staff from sinking into an academic rut.

Cooperation between higher educational establishments and industrial concerns is continually stressed, much of the most important research being conducted as a joint venture between an institute and an industrial plant. The Kalinin Polytechnical Institute in Leningrad, for example, is currently cooperating with the electrical industry to find ways of increasing the supply of power in the next twelve years. More surprisingly, the Herzen Pedagogic Institute in the same city was responsible for devising the alloys used in the carburettor of a new kind of tractor recently produced by the Kirov plant. Technical and scientific research is carefully planned throughout the country, with the aim of dovetailing the industrial organizations and the institutes into one integrated scheme. In practice, this often proves rather difficult; research has a habit of not going according to plan. Maintaining such a scheme where the two sides often fail to coordinate requires a good deal of effort. On the other hand, there are obvious advantages in close cooperation between higher education and the national economy, and it also serves to keep educational work 'closer to life', and fulfils the Marxist requirement of the 'unity of theory and practice'.

Organization and Staffing

The head of a VUZ is known as a Rector and is assisted by a Deputy Rector or Protector. They are appointed and dismissed by the U.S.S.R. Ministry of Higher Education, to which they are responsible for the efficient running of the institution. The chief organ for planning and administration is the Academic Council (*Uchonyi soviet*), roughly equivalent to the Senate of a British University. It is chaired by the Rector, and is composed of deputy rectors, heads of faculties and departments, some of the professors, and representatives of the Communist Party, Komsomol, the trade union, and the ministry. Among its duties are the planning of teaching and research, the confirmation of the appointments of lecturers and assistants, the nomination of senior lecturers and professors, and the awarding of higher degrees.

Each institution is divided into faculties (*fakul'tety*), which are more narrowly defined than in Britain. Instead of faculties of Arts or Science, there are faculties of Chemistry, Biology, History, etc. Faculties have their own Academic Councils; these in effect appoint the faculty staff, subject to confirmation from above. Each is headed by a Dean (*Dekan*), selected from among the faculty's professors by the Director and Academic Council of the institution. His duties include planning and coordination of teaching and research within the faculty, the organization of entrance examinations, and the selection, on the basis of final examination results, of graduates for post-diploma study. This administrative work takes up a considerable part of the Dean's time, but carries an extra payment of fifty per cent of his basic salary.

Faculties are subdivided into departments (*kafedry*). The Russian word can also be rendered 'chair', but this is liable to be misleading. A *kafedra*, unlike a Chair in a British University, may have several professors, and is headed by a Departmental Chairman (*Zaveduyushchii kafedroi*) who is usually, though not necessarily, a professor. Like the Dean of the Faculty, he is paid extra for administrative duties; he is also expected to do his full share of teaching and research.

Each department deals with a special field within its faculty. For example, the Faculty of Geography in Moscow's Lomonosov State University has fourteen departments: general physical geography, physical geography of the U.S.S.R., physical geography of foreign countries, economic geography of the U.S.S.R., economic geography of foreign countries, geomorphology, geodesy and cartography, hydrology, climatology, botanical geography, soil geography, palaeogeography, geography of the Arctic, and the history of geography. Not all faculties are so minutely subdivided; in the Leningrad Herzen Pedagogic Institute, the Faculty of Foreign Languages has four departments,

English, German, French, and Spanish, while the History Faculty has only two – General History and History of the U.S.S.R.

Departmental staffs vary in numbers and composition, but can include up to four or five professors, who usually hold a Doctor's degree; readers or senior lecturers (*dotsenty*), mostly with Candidate degrees; lecturers (*prepodavateli*, literally instructors), and assistant lecturers (*assistenty*). There may also be a number of research specialists (*sotrudniki*) without teaching duties, and, where applicable, laboratory technicians, demonstrators, and the like. Appointments are made by the institute's Academic Council after advertising in the Press, and require confirmation by the Ministry of Higher Education for the posts of reader or professor. All academic staff formally give up their posts every five years; their appointments are in practice nearly always renewed, but the alternative remains a theoretical possibility to prevent staff from atrophying through inactivity.

Future Developments

Prediction is always hazardous, even in a country such as the U.S.S.R. which plans its educational and economic development years in advance. As has been shown by the changes of 1958, 1964, and 1966, forecasts can fail to work out and lines of policy may alter. Nevertheless, a number of trends can be discerned for the immediate future in Soviet higher education.

Expansion is likely to continue, both in response to the needs of the economy and the growing pressure for places. Since higher education is particularly expensive, and since money is always short, part-time courses will continue to account for a substantial proportion of all students. Just how big a part they should play is likely to be a matter for controversy. Apart from financial considerations, they help to mitigate to some extent the keenness of the competition for places; on the other hand, as we have seen, there is some disquiet about the general standard, and concern over the high drop-out rate. There is much talk of the need to improve the work of the higher institutions, especially in the part-time sector, and it is possible that some of the present efforts may bear fruit; but it is also fairly clear, on present trends at any rate, that the proportion of part-time students will decrease.

More emphasis will be placed on research and its integration with the national economy. In 1962 the State Planning Commission put into action a scheme whereby 1,000 research posts a year were to be made available for members of the teaching staffs of institutions to work for doctorate theses 'on pressing theoretical and applied problems'. Institutions have also been empowered to release staff from teaching duties for up to two years if the importance of their research warrants it, to second staff on full pay to industrial research establishments, and to increase the number of post-graduate places, especially for students seconded by their factories or collective farms. Since teaching duties will also become more pressing with the expansion of the institutes, an all-round increase of staff will be called for.

It is extremely unlikely that the expansion of VUZ places will come anywhere near to coping with the increasing number of eligible applicants from the secondary schools. The present gap is more likely to widen than diminish. This could mean a raised standard of academic ability among entrants, but it seems that the authorities are determined, for social and political reasons, not to make this the sole criterion for entry, as can be seen from the emphasis laid on practical work experience, character references, and the like. This pressure for entry, and the continued pressure and weeding-out throughout the entire course, is likely to leave little place for the political waverer, the leisurely scholar, or the '*byeloruchki*' (white-handed) disdainful of manual or applied work. This, at least, is the aim of the authorities though it remains to be seen how far they will be successful. There are signs, however, that many Soviet educationists are alarmed at the sheer weight of cramming and memorizing called for in most courses; if their concern leads to action, this may result in the amount of prescribed reading becoming a little more realistic. Even so, it is likely to remain formidable, and the Soviet student will continue to have a busy time. There are signs, too, that many educationists are unenthusiastic about the scholastic effects of the long work periods, however socially admirable the idea may be.

In certain theoretical fields, such as mathematics and physics, little attention is paid to this requirement, a tendency which may well spread in the future, at least in the pure sciences. Some time will have to go by before it can be seen how successful the attempt has been to integrate practical and academic work in all branches of Soviet higher education.

6. Teachers

Training

Teacher training in the U.S.S.R., as in many continental countries, is still based on separate institutions for different grades of
teacher. On the whole, teachers of secondary school classes
(classes IV to X) are given a full higher education at a university
or pedagogic institute, while those for the elementary classes
(classes I to III) and for the pre-school stages receive their training at specialized secondary schools. The whole structure of
teacher training has been subject to continual reorganization
since 1952, the trend being to reduce the number of different
kinds of institution. In the near future, it is claimed, all schoolteachers will have a full higher educational course; at the present
time, however, this process is not complete, and though the
separation of primary and secondary training is not as clear-cut
as it was, it still remains. Over sixty-seven per cent of all class
teachers now hold higher educational qualifications, and less
than twenty-four per cent have come from pedagogic and other
secondary specialized schools. But there are still nine per cent
who trained at teachers' institutes of a type that was abolished
more than a couple of decades ago. This is a useful reminder of
the obvious but often forgotten fact that changes in the training
system can take a long time to make themselves felt in the
structure of the profession. For the moment, then, teachers receive their basic training at three different types of institutions –
pedagogic schools, pedagogic institutes, and universities.

Teachers

Pedagogic Schools (Pedagogicheskie uchilishcha)

It is still possible for pupils to leave the general school at the end of the eighth form and go directly into teacher training. This is carried on in the *pedagogic schools*, which offer two main types of course: four years for teachers of the elementary classes (I–III) of the general school, and three and a half years for kindergarten teachers. In the major cities there are separate institutions for the two types, but in the country as a whole it is still common for the two to be found together in the same school. In addition, some pedagogic schools train teachers of singing, drawing, physical education and work-training for the primary schools; these courses are available in less than a third of the total number.

In European Russia and the western republics the overwhelming majority of the students are girls, but in some other areas, especially in the Central Asian republics, where many features of the Muslim tradition still survive, the proportion of males can be as high as forty per cent. But this is untypical of the country as a whole; girls account for no less than eighty-nine per cent of all pedagogic school students.[1] Since the mid-1950s, there has been a growing tendency (as with other specialized secondary schools) for students to complete general secondary schooling first and then go on to the pedagogic schools for a two- or three-year course, full- or part-time. But this development is not yet complete, and many students still enter at fifteen.

Since the courses aim to achieve the same standard of general education as the ten-year schools and provide teacher training at the same time, it is not surprising that the curriculum is heavily loaded. As well as the normal general educational subjects (including foreign languages, sciences, etc.), the students have to take teaching methods, psychology, pedagogy, history of pedagogy, music, and drawing. Teaching practice starts in the first year with the observation of lessons in the school attached to the institute; later, the students are taken to ordinary schools where they watch demonstration lessons and discuss them with their tutors. Continuous teaching practice comes later, under the supervision of school directors.

Compared with the pedagogic institutes, the pedagogic schools are generally held to give rather a superficial course, and it is also felt that the students are usually not mature enough. These schools, however, are regarded as temporary expedients; since the 1950s, it has been official policy to get rid of them gradually, and pass their functions over to higher educational institutions; in the meantime, they should concentrate more on the training of kindergarten teachers.

This has not happened yet; indeed, there has been a slight increase recently in the number of pedagogic schools. In the early 1960s, a start was made on phasing them out, but it was soon found in many places that the higher institutes could not provide the extra numbers needed – and this in a situation where the school system was expanding all the time and there was a general teacher shortage in any case. Some of the pedagogic schools have therefore been re-opened, and their abolition has been put off for the time being. Nor have they gone over completely to training kindergarten teachers. As usual, this process has been furthest advanced in the major cities, in some of which primary teacher training at this level has all but disappeared and been replaced by the appropriate courses in the pedagogic institutes. But in the country as a whole there is still some way to go; for many years now, the talk has been of the need to improve the pedagogic schools since it appears that they will be needed for some time yet. Some of the more advanced republics, such as Georgia, Armenia, Estonia, and Latvia, have long since transferred all primary training to the higher institutes; for the rest, the pedagogic schools are regarded as a temporary expedient, to be made as good as possible while 'striving to replace them'. The future of teacher training, it is said, must lie with the higher institutes.[2]

Pedagogic Institutes (*Pedagogicheskie instituty*)

Pedagogic institutes have been growing in numbers and importance over the past decade. Originally, they trained only specialist teachers for the upper forms of the secondary schools; in 1952, they absorbed the Teachers' Institutes, which provided staff for the lower forms; and now they are gradually taking over the functions of the pedagogic schools as well. Courses are for four or five years' duration for secondary teachers, depending on their subjects; in the faculty for primary and pre-school teachers, the course lasts for four years.

Entrance to pedagogic institutes is by competitive examination, character reference, and priority placing. The competition is keen: about one third of all applicants is admitted. Many successful applicants have, as elsewhere in the higher educational system, done two or three years' practical work, although much less is made of this than was the case some years ago. Some of those with work experience come from factories, farms, or the armed forces, but many are graduates of pedagogic schools who have taught primary classes for two or three years and now want to improve their qualifications.

Like other colleges of higher education, pedagogic institutes are divided into faculties catering for the various special fields. These differ slightly from place to place, but those of the Herzen Institute in Leningrad show the general pattern. This college has twelve faculties: (1) Russian language and literature; (2) history, U.S.S.R. and General; (3) mathematics and technical drawing; (4) physics; (5) electrotechnology; (6) biology (with chemistry, oddly enough, as a subsidiary department); (7) foreign languages (with departments of English, French, German, and Spanish); (8) geography; (9) art; (10) sport and physical culture; (11) defectology (which trains specialist teachers for the schools for the physically and mentally handicapped); (12) pedagogy. The courses in all faculties last for five years, except those in physical culture and pedagogy, which are only four years. The last-named faculty is at present expanding to take over from the pedagogic schools. This Institute is unusual in having a special 'Northern Department', which trains students from various Arctic minorities for general teaching among their own peoples. In contains thirty-seven different nationalities, with about half a dozen students from each.

The curriculum of the pedagogic institutes can be divided into three main areas: political and general courses common to all students everywhere, educational theory, and the special subjects.

The political courses call for little comment, since they are substantially the same as those in the universities and elsewhere. They take up a slightly smaller proportion of the time than in a university, but the difference is tiny. As we have seen, the time given to these courses is greater than that set aside for educational theory, which may be taken as an indication of the seriousness with which the political side of teacher preparation is taken. General courses include sport, physical education, and a foreign language; altogether they take up not much more than six per cent of the curriculum.

The courses in educational theory are obligatory for students, and account for between thirteen and twenty per cent of the time in most cases. The main items here are psychology (mainly Pavlovian, though some psychoanalytic doctrines, such as those of Freud, make an occasional if brief appearance; mental testing techniques are, of course, not taught); pedagogy (educational theory in the widest sense, ranging from general educational aims to problems of moral education, discipline, etc.); history of pedagogy, including some comparative education; and general principles of teaching method. There are also subsidiary courses in school hygiene, films and visual aids, the running of extra-curricular activities, and the like.

Special subjects make up the major elements of the course, amounting to about forty per cent in most specialities, sometimes more – for language teachers it is over seventy per cent. When the length of course was increased from four to five years in 1956, students were required to qualify in two or more special subjects, not one. The main groups were as follows: (1) mathematics and physics; (2) mathematics and technical drawing; (3) physics and fundamentals of production; (4) biology, chemistry, and fundamentals of agriculture; (5) geography and biology; (6) two foreign languages; (7) Russian language and literature with history; and so on. Facilities were also made available for students to take additional qualifications (such as art or music for elementary classes) through 'circles' organized by the institute. One reason for broadening the course in this way was that it had been found exceedingly difficult to staff rural schools adequately with single-

Teachers

subject specialists; on the other hand, complaints about overloading of students were not slow in coming. In 1963, the courses
were reduced again to four years and one special subject,[3] a
measure which met the complaints about overwork but left the
supply problem as it was. Since then, compromise has crept in; it
is now possible for students to opt either to qualify in one speciality in four years, or two in five years. (The subject groupings are
much the same as before, with some minor variations.) The
majority, in practice, prefer the five-year double course, though
the criticisms – and the basis for them – have not vanished.

Teaching practice, amounting to a total of between sixteen and
nineteen weeks, starts in the third or fourth year. As in the
pedagogic schools, it begins in a modest way with the observation
and discussion of lessons, and works up to continuous periods of
teaching in an ordinary school, with occasional supervision by the
head. These continuous periods may be spent in local schools,
but since there are often not enough of them in the town to take
all the students, many may have to practise in rural schools far
from the institutes. Teaching practice is elaborately planned to
include preparatory seminars in the institute, observation of all
lessons taken by the class to which the student is assigned,
participation in extra-curricular activities, conducting a number
of psychological case-studies of pupils, planning a series of
lessons and teaching some of them under supervision, evaluation
seminars at the end of the practice period, and so on. It does not
always work out quite like this, however; in areas where teacher
shortage is still a problem, students are sometimes simply given
a timetable and told to get on with it. It is less common now to
hear the complaints, frequent in the mid-1960s, that in many
areas the programme of teaching practice had been 'effectively
liquidated', but it still does happen from time to time.[4] In addition to this, students must put in three weeks in the summer
vacation after their third year as youth leaders at a Pioneer camp.
This training for extra-curricular work is regarded as an important part of their course. As an official of one institute put it,
'They have to learn not only to be teachers of special subjects,
but teachers of children as well.' Considering the important role

156

of the youth movement in the entire educational system, this emphasis is only to be expected.

Universities

It is possible in the U.S.S.R., as it once was in England, to go into teaching direct from a university without further training of any kind. Unlike the English universities, however, those of the U.S.S.R. prepare for this by including pedagogic subjects, teaching methods, and teaching practice in the basic course, whether the student has declared an intention of going into teaching or not. Officially, the universities are supposed to direct into teaching a high proportion of their graduates annually – sixty per cent of the mathematicians, physicists, and chemists, and no less than eighty per cent of their biologists, geographers, historians, and 'philologists' (i.e. graduates in Russian and foreign languages). In fact, a far smaller number than this is sent into the schools, and many of those who are directed fail to appear.

The universities contribute only a minority of recruits to the teaching profession, compared with the other colleges. Proportions fluctuate, but the number of new teachers from the pedagogic institutes can be as much as eight times as great as that from the universities. Proportionately small though this may seem, it is still a large number, and the universities can be considered an important source of teachers.

The training given at the universities has the same general outlines as at the pedagogic institutes, but the emphasis is rather different. Students there spent, as we have seen, rather more time on the political subjects, while the pedagogic courses are less prominent – little more than half in most cases. There is also less teaching practice, amounting to no more than two months altogether. Study of the special subject, on the other hand, is a good deal deeper; students in the universities have to offer only one speciality, compared with two or three in the pedagogic institute. In spite of the official equality of standing of the two types of establishment, it is generally felt that there is a real gap – one claimed to be narrowing, but a gap none the less. On average, the university graduate is about a year ahead of his institute-trained colleague as a subject specialist, but is liable to be a less competent teacher and less well versed in educational theory. There are also frequent complaints about the motivation of university graduates in teaching; a commentator who called them 'temporary sojourners in the educational field who gleefully quit the schools at the first opportunity' was typical of many who felt that the commitment of many university graduates to their job left a good deal to be desired, and wondered if the universities were really suitable training-grounds for teachers at all.[5] But the more usual view is that the schools need both types, one with the advantage of breadth and the other of depth; this seems to be the official position also.

In-Service Training, Advanced Courses, and Research

Institutes for Teacher Improvement

The undoubted problems of initial teacher training in the U.S.S.R. are offset to a considerable extent by the fact that training does not end when the teacher leaves college or university and enters the classroom. Great importance is attached to in-service training, which is provided by an extensive network of Teacher Improvement Institutes (*Instituty usovershenstvovaniya uchitelei*), which organize regular refresher courses and also act as advisory centres. The first of these was opened in Moscow in 1938, and the system has expanded since then to reach every part of the country. The Moscow institute is the largest, with a specialist full-time staff of sixty-five (plus the part-time services of teachers from the higher institutes) in twenty departments (*kabinety*), and a subsidiary centre in every district of the city. Its regular courses are attended by 10,000 teachers each year; and a further 30,000 make use of its advisory services or attend special lectures on subjects of topical importance, such as a new law or major curricular change. There are over a hundred such institutes in the U.S.S.R. as a whole.

Teachers are now required to take in-service courses every five years; these were formerly voluntary, but now that there are enough facilities for all, this is now a condition of continued employment. There are different forms, but the most usual – in the towns at any rate – is full-time day release, twice a week, every fifth year. The courses cover three major areas: (1) Marxist–Leninist philosophy, with particular reference to its application to the teachers' own subjects and the educational process generally; (2) subject content, with particular emphasis on new developments (this is regarded as especially important in mathematics and the science subjects, where new schemes of work are being introduced to take account of the expansion of knowledge; and (3) teaching methods. This last area is affected not only by technical developments (increasing use of audio-visual aids, programmed learning, etc.), but by a shift in emphasis from 'chalk-and-talk' class teaching to more work with individuals and small groups within the class, which requires a greater flexibility and sophistication than has hitherto been either possible or necessary. Teachers on release for in-service courses are still paid their full salary, and the schools are staffed so as to allow for a proportion of teachers being absent for this purpose at any given time. (This has always been policy, but local shortages of teachers have made it difficult to implement it in some places until recently, and there are still one or two areas where practical problems of staffing inhibit the proper working of the in-service training system.)

In remote areas, full-time day-release courses are rarely practicable, and other methods have to be used. In extreme cases, correspondence courses (topped up with short residential seminars) have to be used; but in the less thinly populated parts of the country, one-month residential courses are provided instead. Alternatively, where conditions permit, members of the staff of the nearest institute may travel to a centrally-placed larger village and teach one-day courses for the teachers of the surrounding area. This involves the expense of travel to the institute and a good deal of inconvenience to the individuals concerned, but it seems to be preferred to residential courses which, although possibly more effective in some ways, are both more expensive for the authorities and more inconvenient for teacher and taught alike. The *way* in which teachers take in-service training is tailored to local conditions, and is thought to be relatively unimportant; but it is seen as absolutely vital that they should do so somehow. As the director of one institute put it, 'The teacher who ceases to learn has ceased to be a teacher.'[6]

The Improvement Institutes deal with other things than in-service courses, though these remain by far their most important function. They run monthly seminars for school directors. (Future heads and assistant heads have to take a two-month full-time course of training in the year before they take up office, but this is a function of the pedagogic institutes rather than the improvement institutes.) They organize special courses and conferences, provide consultancy services for teachers with problems in teaching techniques, sometimes taking these out to the schools rather than waiting for the teachers to come to them. (These are popularly known as 'teachers' ambulances'.) There are departments of extra-curricular work, general educational and specialist libraries, libraries of educational films and other teaching aids, and workshops and laboratories where teachers can try out techniques for themselves. The institutes also produce a flood of pamphlets on methods and other school problems.

Many pedagogic institutes also provide their own refresher courses for teachers in service. The Moscow Pedagogic Institute of Foreign Languages, for example (a specialized establishment which trains interpreters and translators as well as language teachers) has a variety of these. In addition to the 6,000 day and part-time students doing the basic course, there are over a hundred teachers, released from their schools, studying to teach their own special subjects in a foreign language in one of the special 'Language Schools'; six-month improvement courses for language specialists are also given, as well as more advanced two-year full-time courses (with salary) which can lead to a higher teaching diploma.[7]

Post-Graduate Studies

Like other types of VUZ, the pedagogic institutes provide facilities for post-graduate study and research. The normal procedure is for the graduate to take up his teaching duties for two or three years, then apply for admission to the higher courses. The proportion accepted is little more than three per cent of all graduates, though it can be higher in some places such as the Herzen Institute in Leningrad, the Lenin Pedagogic Institute in Moscow, the specialist pedagogic institutes of foreign languages in Gorki, Minsk, and Moscow, or others with particularly strong postgraduate departments. The course lasts for three years of full-time study, the student being paid his full teacher's salary in the meantime. At the end of the third year he presents his thesis in the usual way, and if successful is awarded the degree of Candidate of Pedagogic Sciences (*Kandidat pedagogicheskikh nauk*), which entitles him to a higher salary, to say nothing of the increased prestige. Alternatively, the teacher can study for his higher degree by correspondence for four years, with an additional year of full-time study at the institute to prepare his thesis. All post-graduate students are supervised by a member of the staff of the appropriate department.

Members of the staffs of the institutes are, of course, also expected to conduct research. Occasionally, as we have seen in the previous chapter, this is not always strictly educational, but such cases are exceptions. A few examples from the Herzen Institute in Leningrad will serve to show the kind of research normally carried on. The Department of Pedagogy is working on problems of consciousness in learning, moral education, and polytechnical education, and is planning a textbook of educational theory for use in teacher training, subject to the usual ministerial approval. The Department of History has produced a textbook of English history, now a standard text throughout the R.S.F.S.R.; the various methods departments have written textbooks for a long time, and are now working on the production and improvement of aural and visual teaching aids, which have until recently been something of a Cinderella of the Soviet educational system. As elsewhere, research is planned in advance, stress being laid on cooperation with other departments, institutes and research bodies, and with industry.

The Academy of Pedagogic Sciences

The Academy of Pedagogic Sciences of the U.S.S.R., or A.P.N. (*Akademiya pedagogicheskikh nauk SSSR*) has no precise British equivalent, though such bodies as the Schools Council, the Scottish Council for Research in Education or the National Foundation for Educational Research carry out some of the same functions. Its purpose is to conduct advanced research, to spread educational information among the general public, to train post-graduate students and teachers for the pedagogic institutes, and to act as a general clearing-house for educational studies and discussion. It has an important role to play in the formation of educational policy too; although this rests in the last analysis with the higher echelons of Government and Party, it may rely heavily in the formative stages on the Academy's researches and recommendations. Further, although the broad outlines of policy are laid down from on high, they are generally passed on to the Academy for the working out of details, which puts it in a position to wield considerable influence, and even, on occasion, to bring about substantial modifications in the policy itself; the failure of the special schools for high-fliers in mathematics and science to develop as a major feature of the system is widely believed to be a case in point, though of course this kind of statement is virtually impossible to prove. What cannot be doubted is that the Academy is much more than an arm of the Ministry; it can be a powerful voice in the formulation of policy as well as the working out of detailed practice.

The A.P.N. was founded in 1943, originally as the Academy of Pedagogic Sciences of the R.S.F.S.R. (In the other Republics, Institutes of the Academies of Sciences filled a similar role.) Its influence, however, extended in practice beyond the Russian Federation to the whole of the Union. In 1966, after some strong criticism of 'dispersal of resources' and 'lack of effective links between research and school practice',[8] this situation was formally recognized; the A.P.N. was reorganized on an all-Union basis, and re-named the Academy of Pedagogic Sciences of the U.S.S.R., on the analogy of the Academies of Arts, Medical

Sciences, and the like. The other republics continue to operate their own Institutes of Pedagogy as before.

As in the Royal Society or the Académie Française, members are elected by their fellows, not appointed by any outside body. There are two categories of membership, full members (*deistvitel'nye chleny*) and corresponding members (*chleny-korrespondenty*), both entitled to the rank of 'Academician' ('*Akademik*') and a large extra salary. Membership also brings the holder great prestige, both in educational circles and in society at large. There are 126 academicians at present.

The Academy is made up of a number of special institutes, each devoted to a particular branch of educational research. Examples are the Research Institute for the History and Theory of Pedagogy, the Research Institute of Teaching Methods, the Research Institute of Defectology, the Leningrad Natural Science Institute, the Research Institute of Psychology, the Institute for Education in the non-Russian schools, and so forth. These are subdivided into specialist departments; the first-named, for example, has departments of pre-school education, polytechnical education, history of education, etc., while the Institute of Defectology has departments dealing with the problems of each specific kind of physical and mental defect. Under the Academy's jurisdiction come also the Ushinsky State Library of Education, the National Education Museum in Leningrad, and the Research Archives, a vast collection of research documents and papers by Soviet and foreign educationists.

The regular business of the Academy is run by a Praesidium of about half a dozen full members. This body, apart from routine administration, is responsible for the Bureau for the Study of Foreign Education and the Academy's publishing house, among other things. Through this press a large number of educational journals is issued; among the most important are *Sovietskaya pedagogika* (*Soviet Pedagogy*), *Voprosy psikhologii* (*Problems of Psychology*), and *Semya i shkola* (*Family and School*). To these can be added many textbooks and other educational works. The compilation of a Children's Encyclopedia is still in progress, but will not be complete for some time; a Pedagogic Dictionary appeared many years ago, and a fuller Pedagogic Encyclopedia is now complete. The Academy also sponsors popular lectures on educational topics, and conducts contests ('Pedagogic readings') in which teachers and other educational workers submit reports and studies. The prize-winning entries are subsequently published. Finally, the Academy runs a number of experimental schools, which prove of enormous value to its army of research workers.

The Educational Trade Union

There is now only one union for all teachers in the U.S.S.R.; known as the 'U.S.S.R. Trade Union of Workers in Education, Higher Schools, and Research Establishments' ('*Profsoyuz rabotnikov prosveshcheniya, vysshei shkoly i nauchnykh uchrezhdenii SSSR*'); it is the result of a merger in 1957 of the two separate bodies for school and higher educational staff. Since membership of a Soviet trade union is determined by a person's place of employment rather than his craft or professional qualification, this body includes every school and college worker from an academician to a school cleaner in its current membership of over four million. Twenty per cent of these are said to be members of the Communist Party, a marked contrast to the proportion of party membership in the population at large – about four and a half per cent – and yet another eloquent testimony to the close links between the educational system and the political aims of the Soviet régime. Membership of the union is officially voluntary, but ninety-eight per cent join as soon as they start work, most of the remainder coming in not much later. Subscriptions are not fixed as an absolute sum, but are reckoned at one-half per cent of the member's salary, whatever that may be.

The educational union, like other Soviet trade unions, is not a bargaining body in the Western sense. Its functions do include making representations on pay, pensions, and conditions to the government, but head-on clashes are of course avoided by the fact that the unions are, by virtue of Party control, instruments and not opponents of government policy. It does serve, however, to make teachers' views known, can protect its members from unfair dismissal and bureaucratic interference (sometimes), and helps to enforce regulations on school building, heating, lighting, etc., which are not infrequently evaded, to the teachers' detriment, by local officials.

Much of the union's work is in the field of welfare services for its members. From part of the subscriptions, and other sources, it maintains a social insurance fund which enables teachers to receive full pay during illness, and provides hostels for old or disabled members. It also runs many recreational facilities – clubs, gymnasia, sports-grounds, and the like, and performs other services, such as helping teachers to find accommodation when they take up jobs in new areas.

In conjunction with the Ministry of Education of the U.S.S.R., the union publishes a thrice-weekly newspaper, *Uchitelskaya gazeta* (*The Teachers' Newspaper*). This is in many ways one of the most valuable of its activities, for this paper not only publishes news of interest to teachers, but provides a platform for controversies and complaints, and is frequently instrumental in having grievances put right. Many of the abuses in the system, due to neglect or unwarranted interference by local officials, depend on silence for their continuation; teachers often write to the *Gazeta* to complain of these abuses, and this is often followed by comment in its columns and the dispatch of a reporter to investigate. This is often enough; in the more serious cases an official inquiry may follow, with at least the public apology of the guilty functionary, and even with his demotion, dismissal, or arrest. In one recent case, the headmaster of a rural school, with the connivance of the chairman of the village Soviet (who happened to be his brother-in-law), compelled the schoolchildren to build a garage for him, work in his garden, and perform most of his wife's domestic tasks. Teachers' protests to the local authorities that this was an illegitimate interpretation of 'socially useful labour' were, not surprisingly, of no avail. A letter of complaint was followed by a visit from one of the roving reporters of the *Gazeta*. Before very long, the headmaster and his obliging brother-in-law were both removed from their positions and publicly denounced in ringing terms, though nothing worse seems to have happened to them.

Comparatively few of the grievances dealt with are as serious as this, but the misplaced enthusiasm of Party officials often needs intervention of this kind to provide a remedy. One complaint in 1962 came from six rural teachers in the Tatar Republic, alleging that they had been dragooned into agricultural work in their spare time by the local Party Secretary, and had been called back from their holidays to help with the harvest. The *Gazeta* pointed out that this was totally illegal, and drew the matter to the attention of higher authorities, who promptly put a stop to the practice and rapped the over-zealous official over the knuckles. Complaints about staffing, overloading of timetables, shortage of housing for teachers, excessive demands on extra-curricular time, problems about holiday pay, and many other such matters are aired in the paper's columns. Usually, too, it can be announced within a short time that the situation has been put right. How far this is an indication of the paper's effectiveness as a righter of wrongs, and how far the likelihood of remedy determines what complaints are published in the first place, is a matter for speculation. Some observers have compared the role of *Uchitel'skaya gazeta* to that of the *Ombudsman* in Scandinavia. This is true up to a point – the paper does put forward complaints and takes steps to put them right. The comparison is exaggerated, however, because the *Ombudsman* is an independent agent, while the *Gazeta* is not. It would not get very far, for instance, in dealing with grievances that the central authorities were unable or unwilling to rectify. Nevertheless, there can be little doubt that teachers in difficulties often find a valuable ally in *Uchitelskaya gazeta*.

Teaching Loads and Class Size

The basic working week for a Soviet teacher consists of eighteen hours in the secondary classes (forms IV to XI), twenty-four hours for primary classes (forms I to III). Any extra time is paid for at the appropriate rate. As in most Continental countries, teachers are free to go when not actually on duty. Most teachers in fact put in more than the basic number of hours – just how much more depends on the local staffing situation. In the cities, for example, between twenty and twenty-five hours a week is the average load in most secondary subjects; in some rural areas, on the other hand, there are still local staffing difficulties, and teachers at the same stage may find themselves doing thirty hours a week or more. In spite of the extra pay, this is far from welcome, to judge from complaints appearing regularly in the *Uchitel'skaya gazeta*.

Demands on a teacher's time go beyond actual classwork. All are expected, as a matter of policy, to visit the homes of their pupils, attend parent–teacher meetings, take some part in extra-curricular work, and so forth. Where staff is adequate, these extras are not unduly burdensome, but where there is a shortage, the extra duties as well as the teaching load can pile up alarmingly. One extreme case (presumably extreme, since it was the subject of outraged complaint by the lady's husband) that was recently brought to light concerned a chemistry teacher in Minsk: apart from a teaching load of twenty-two hours, her regular activities (most of them weekly) included a political seminar, a class-teacher's period, a meeting of the Teachers' Soviet, the school's chemistry 'circle', meetings with the Parents' Committee, 'School Evenings', and so forth. This may not be typical in extent, but complaints about excessive demands on time are frequent; clearly many officials have failed to appreciate that teachers have homes of their own and that time is not elastic.

Size of classes and pupil–teacher ratios again vary considerably from place to place. The national average pupil–teacher ratio is seventeen to one, the average class thirty or more strong, but again there is a discrepancy between town and country. The more remote areas, as usual, come off worst – one reason for the frequent delays in changing over from seven-year to eight-year schooling in some parts; it is difficult to get sufficient staff to cope with the increase in the number of pupils. Even in the more favoured areas, classes still tend to be large. It is possible that the formal manner of teaching makes class numbers matter less than they would if activity methods were more in vogue.

School Directors

The Head of a school (just as likely to be a woman as a man) is not merely its chief administrative officer; he is required to take a proportion of the regular teaching duties as well, to keep in touch with the classes by regularly observing his staff at work, and to be a 'model teacher' into the bargain by giving advice and taking demonstration lessons from time to time. In view of his other duties, his maximum teaching load is usually twelve hours a week; this may be increased in exceptional circumstances (such as a particularly acute staff shortage), but even then the absolute maximum is eighteen hours a week.

On top of this he has a considerable amount of organizational work – timetabling, planning excursions, filling forms and making returns, chairing meetings of the school's Pedagogic Council, attending Parents' Committee meetings, interviewing problem children and their parents, helping to find accommodation for his staff in rural areas, and so on. In country areas the extra work is liable to spill over into a variety of activities outside the school, for the director is often (like the old Scottish dominie) a leading member of the community by virtue of his position and intellectual standing. This has the advantage of making him a locally influential figure, but he is also expected to play a leading part in local affairs, with consequent heavy demands on his time. One country headmaster, whose burden seems not unusual, wrote to the *Uchitel'skaya gazeta* that he was 'overwhelmed with meetings, deliberations, and journeys', listing some of the duties he was expected to perform in addition to his normal teaching and school administrative work: as a prominent local worthy he had been elected to both the village Soviet and the Soviet of the nearby town, and had to attend their meetings, and those of their executive committees, as well as educational seminars, meetings of heads of schools, and the like. He did not question his duty to pull his weight in community affairs, but felt that things had gone too far, adding that he avoided the telephone in case some new series of meetings would call for his presence. Once again, overloading of this kind seems much heavier in the rural areas, where teachers and intellectuals generally are much thinner on the ground. City directors may still have extra duties, in school and out, but on a more moderate scale.

A director's powers are in some respects less extensive than those of the headmaster in a British school. Although he is entitled to see that teachers are complying with the regulation schemes of work and teaching methods, he is not apparently entitled to order one teacher to take the class of another who is absent. Any intervention he makes in a class-teachers' work can be subject to an appeal to the Teacher's Soviet. One rather odd example of this was reported in *Uchitel'skaya gazeta*. A pupil had handed in an essay on the poetry of Mayakovsky; although this poet is highly thought of officially and generally, the pupil's assessment of his talents was severely critical, to put it mildly. Scandalized, the teacher awarded it a mark of 2, the second lowest possible, whereupon the pupil appealed to the director. He liked it and remarked it as a 5, the highest possible. This time the teacher appealed to the Teacher's Soviet, which compromised with a 3. The report of this incident was followed by a spate of letters on one side or the other, no official comment being made;[9] the significant thing is that nobody questioned the right to appeal in either case. In general, the director's powers, compared with those of his counterpart in this country, are limited on the one hand by the high degree of central control in the educational system, and on the other hand by his staff through their various committees. In this, the Soviet Union is closer to the international norm; the amount of power given to individual heads in England and Wales (and to a lesser extent in Scotland) astonishes many observers, from Western countries as well as the U.S.S.R. or Eastern Europe – particularly since they see little evidence of an adequate system of training heads for the exercise of this power.

Salaries and Pensions

It is well-nigh impossible to make any realistic comparison between teachers' salaries in the U.S.S.R. and in this country. For one thing, the official exchange rate is completely artificial, as anyone who has been pestered by touts on Red Square to exchange money at two to three times the official rate (and, of course, quite illegally) will realize all too well. For another, exchange rates fluctuate so quickly that there is little point in trying to pin them down here. But there is a more fundamental difficulty: living costs and wage structures in the U.S.S.R. and here are so different that any translation of costs is likely to be highly misleading. For many basic goods, Soviet costs are higher than in the United Kingdom, and it can be said, with reasonable accuracy, that even in the cities the standard of living is substantially lower than in the West. But the detailed picture is more confusing. Many commodities that take up a major part of our spending, such as cars, refrigerators, washing machines, and the like, are very expensive and difficult to come by; and by any standards other items such as adults' clothing, shoes, and some foods must be reckoned expensive. Yet the commonest complaints are not so much about shortage of cash as the lack of anything to buy – hence the eagerness of many Soviet citizens to buy visitors' jeans and drip-dry shirts (or currency, which can be used to buy scarce consumer goods in the 'Byeryozka' foreign-currency shops). Some basic items are, in fact, very cheap, such as rent, heating and lighting, and public transport; so are most 'cultural goods' like books, records, and theatre tickets, which are deliberately kept down in price for exactly the same reason that the cost of cigarettes and spirits (as opposed to wines) has been raised – price structures are being used as an instrument of the government's social policies. Also, since the vast majority of married women carry on with their jobs, wage policies are based on the assumption that the typical household has at least two salaries coming in. Against this background, the least misleading generalization would be that a teacher's salary in the middle of the range is roughly comparable with that of a skilled worker in industry, and that within the school system (counting heads of schools but not higher education staff) the highest salaries can rise to about three or four times the basic minimum.

Soviet teachers' salaries depend on a number of factors, the most important of which are:

1. The teacher's educational qualification. The highest basic rate is for graduates of higher educational institutions, irrespective of the kind of institution attended (university, pedagogic institute, or any other). The rates are lower for those who have qualified at a pedagogic school or other secondary specialized school. There are also separate scales for graduates of the old *teachers' institutes* (these have long ceased to exist, but there are still a few of their graduates in the system), which come in between the other two. A lower scale exists for teachers who have only general school education, but there are hardly any of these left in the schools now; they are survivors of a time when the shortage of teachers made it impossible to insist on the legal qualifications in all schools, especially in remote areas.

2. Length of service. Unlike our system of a regular scale of annual incremental increases, Soviet salaries appear to go up by bigger but less frequent jumps – after five, ten, and twenty-five years, finishing with about one and a half times the original figure.

3. Location of the school. Extra payments are made for teaching in certain remote areas. These can be quite substantial – twenty per cent in the Yakut Republic (a northern subdivision of the R.S.F.S.R.) and part of Irkutsk province, and fifty per cent extra (plus periodic leave on full salary to more central parts) for teaching in Kamchatka or Sakhalin in the Far East or in the northern tribal areas. Until 1964, teachers were paid more in the towns than in the country, as rural teachers were entitled to free housing, heating and lighting and a plot of land for their own use, according to the practice of the local collective or state farm. (There were many complaints, however, that being entitled legally to these benefits was one thing, but getting them out of the collective farm committee could sometimes be quite another.) The differential was not large, and was abolished in 1964 in an attempt to induce more teachers to go to the rural areas. The law of 15 July 1964 also raised salaries generally, and abolished other differentials according to the level of class taught.

Additional salary can be paid on a number of grounds, the most important of which are: (1) Overtime; any extra teaching over the basic minimum of eighteen hours a week in secondary and twenty-four in primary classes is paid at the rate of one-eighteenth and one twenty-fourth of the weekly salary for every such lesson. Most teachers in fact do this, though the opportunities are much greater in the secondary classes (as well as being paid at higher rates). (2) The holding of higher degrees, such as Candidate of Pedagogic Sciences, or for the award of such titles as 'Honoured Teacher'.[10] (3) Holding posts of responsibility, such as school director, assistant director, class adviser, etc. As in the U.K., the actual amount depends on the size of the school (and is greater still in boarding schools), but the differentials are not so large. The head of a large boarding school earning three and a half times the salary of a newly qualified teacher is something of an exception; the director of a large day school making something over twice the salary of a beginner gives a better picture of the effective range. (4) Marking exercises, etc. This is a small flat-rate payment which varies slightly according to the subject; more is paid for marking essays in Russian literature, for example, than for correcting mathematical problems, presumably because this is considered more difficult and time-consuming. (5) Setting up and checking laboratory equipment, taking care of experimental plots, acting as school librarian – these all bring small but useful additional payments. (6) Teaching in a foreign language in a school where the language is used as the medium of instruction.

Holiday pay is calculated not on the basic salary, but on average actual earnings, including extra payments such as overtime. Pensions, amounting to forty per cent of the full salary, are payable at the end of twenty-five years' service; a teacher who carries on working is entitled to full salary and pension as well.

Even allowing for the fact that wages in the U.S.S.R. are on the whole a good deal lower than in the U.K., and for the fact that incomes (for reasons mentioned above) give an incomplete picture anyway, it is still difficult to regard the salaries of most teachers as an adequate recognition of the teacher's worth to society. Proclamations to the effect that the success of educational policies depend 'wholly and utterly upon the teacher' are common,[11] as are the demands on the time of individual teachers for a wide range of social and political activities. But the rewards in hard cash are less impressive. At the upper end of the scale, they can be high – the senior staff of higher educational institutions, academicians, directors with higher qualifications, and teachers who write textbooks[12] can do very well financially; but for the ordinary classroom teacher, especially at the beginning of his or her career, the salary is still modest despite recent improvements.

Social Status of the Teacher

Learning and scholarship in old Russian were traditionally regarded with reverence bordering on superstition, especially by those who lacked them. The teacher, as the 'intellectual' with whom people were most likely to come in contact, was looked on with particular esteem, tempered in some cases with suspicion. After the revolution their prestige diminished considerably; socially, industrial work gained status at the expense of intellectual activity, and politically teachers as a group were suspected of being tarred with the bourgeois brush. The influx of new ill-trained teachers to the schools and colleges did not help matters either.

It was not long before the Soviet régime realized the importance of education for the realization of its ends; the standard of teacher training was raised as soon as possible, and teachers were given continuous propaganda boosts by the authorities. Both processes have gone on since the 1930s; among a welter of official proclamations, two quotations from *Pravda* will serve to show the official attitude: 'The many changes which have occurred in our Motherland under the Soviet régime are in no small degree due to the selfless labour of the Soviet teacher' (December 1954). A headline in July 1960 is more precise: 'The teacher is the closest aid of the Party in rearing the New Man'. Respect for the teacher has long been held up by the authorities as a political and social virtue.

Apart from sloganizing, one way in which the government gives recognition to the work of teachers is by awarding them honours and decorations. Some of these are specifically educational, such as 'Honoured Teacher of the R.S.F.S.R.', but educational workers account for a high proportion of the general Soviet 'Honours List'. The American George Counts, writing in 1961,[13] details the presentation to teachers of the highest state decorations, including 86 Orders of Lenin, 163 Orders of the Red Banner of Labour, 258 Orders of the Badge of Honour, and 697 Medals for Labour Valour. Some of the Orders of Lenin (the highest award in the U.S.S.R.) went to such leading figures as the Minister of Education of the R.S.F.S.R., the President of the Academy of Pedagogic Sciences, and other 'top brass', but even at this level schoolteachers and directors figured prominently.

Popular attitudes are more difficult to judge. There are instances of parent-teacher bodies finding it difficult to arouse interest among the local populace, or of students who regard teaching as a second-best job (and not only for financial reasons), or parents in some of the more remote Central Asian areas who regard teachers as sinister government agents who introduce all manner of modern devilry such as making girls go to school. The old automatic respect, where it depended on the reverence of the ignorant for the learned, was bound to dwindle with the growth of mass education. The average teacher's financial status, above all, is hardly likely to raise his prestige in the eyes of his fellow-citizens. Governmental pronouncements notwithstanding, it is probable that the status of the profession has not yet fully recovered from the collapse of the 1930s.

On the other hand, the social prestige of the teacher has risen. Politically, they are supported at all levels; socially, they play a part in local and national affairs out of all proportion to their numbers. The level of teachers' qualifications is improving, which is likely to increase their prestige. Education is also the most important road to advancement, which enhances the teacher's standing in the eyes of pupils and parents alike. Traditional regard for 'culture' helps too; the popular awe of the teacher as the fount of all wisdom was bound to vanish, but this does not mean that he can be dismissed as of no account. The present wage levels can hardly be called tempting, yet competition for entry to the pedagogic institutes is keen. Popular respect for education is high; the Soviet Union as a whole appears to value its teachers at least in the abstract. If the authorities were to back up their statements with cash, they would leave the teachers in no doubt at all of their importance to the community and the nation.

7. Conclusions and Comments

The non-communist observer of the Soviet educational system is faced with the basic difficulty that many of his own standards of judgement on educational matters do not apply. The system is expressly designed to help in the building of a communist society, and is carefully controlled by the Soviet state and the Communist Party for that purpose. Its success or failure is judged largely by the extent to which it seems likely to assist those social and political ends. Basically, then, the outside observer's view of Soviet education must depend on his view of the U.S.S.R., and inevitably involves the discussion of wider issues than the strictly educational. Important though these issues are, this is not the place for a critique of Marxist theory or its Leninist adaptations as currently applied in the Soviet Union. The educational system of any country has to be examined in its context; it is one thing to object to Communism, or Catholicism, or 'Americanism', but quite another to object to the fact that the schools of certain countries seek to propagate Marxism, Catholic doctrine, or the American Way of Life. It is hard to see how they could do anything else. There is little point in condemning a chisel for not being a screwdriver.

When all that is allowed for, comments can still be made on Soviet education within its own terms of reference. It is only to be expected that it will adopt a Marxist–Leninist viewpoint, and seek to build a new society by training the 'New Man'; but it is still open to question whether a dogmatic approach can serve the interests of any society other than the most static. A growing number of thoughtful Marxists in the Soviet Union have been expressing such doubts with increasing candour, and have there-

by incurred the wrath of the authorities, with its attendant un-
pleasant consequences; but they are well within a strong tradition
in Marxism itself. Marx once said himself that he would never
become a Marxist; Engels was careful to point out that Marxism
was not a doctrine, but a method of inquiry; Sidney and Beatrice
Webb, warm admirers of the U.S.S.R. in most respects, still felt
it necessary in 1935 to warn about the dangers of what they called
'the disease of orthodoxy'.[1] Yet there has always been a strong
tendency in the U.S.S.R. to regard Marxism–Leninism in its
current official interpretation as a kind of Holy Writ; the solutions to problems of the twentieth century are often presupposed
by reference to the statements of a philosopher of the nineteenth.
Dogmatism and heresy-hunting are less widespread, and the
penalties for deviation are less drastic, than in the heyday of
Lysenko and Zhdanov during the Stalin era, but recent events
have shown forcibly that they are by no means gone; thaw has
been followed by freeze again and again, and the bullying of
writers and artists, civil rights campaigners, and of workers
trying to have abuses redressed (even when their actions are
not in breach of Soviet law and when they are demanding no more
than the rights they are supposed to enjoy under the Constitution) does the reputation of the Soviet Union no good at all. In
education, the same danger is present, especially at the higher
levels; the notion that investigation and experiment must fit the
facts to the theory is profoundly unscientific. This has been
recognized to some extent in the scientific field; scientists have
been left relatively free of ideological blinkers (as long as they
stick to science), and it may be of some significance that it is here
that the Soviet Union's greatest successes have been achieved.
It remains for the same point to be taken concerning philosophy,
history, and the arts, though the prospects for an easing-off here
seem far from bright at the moment. The Soviet authorities
would not, of course, be impressed in the slightest by any argument that education and its content should be free of political
control and ideological guidance; indeed, they would consider
this a total impossibility. But they might consider that when the
Marxist framework of ideas is allowed to become a cage, limita-

tions are placed on creativity and constructive thinking which no growing society in a rapidly changing world can afford.

The same holds good for the approach to moral education. In the circumstances, it is only to be expected that it should be based on political, social, and patriotic virtues, and that the schools should seek to instil these from the earliest possible moment. The seriousness with which the problem is taken, and the important place given to it in school and teacher-training programmes, is something that merits our close attention. Further, it does seem to work to some extent, if the high level of cooperation in the schools is anything to go by. Just how far it is successful in the long run is impossible to judge, but clearly it is far from wholly effective. The continual sloganizing on moral matters appears to have little effect on the growing number of juvenile delinquents; with others, preaching can lead to indifference and even outright rebellion. For all the stress on moral education, graft and corruption have long been prominent features in many sections of Soviet society. This had become so serious by the early 1960s that the death penalty was actually introduced for economic crimes, a pretty clear example of a panic measure; but the roots go deep. Even government departments have been known to make use of the ubiquitous 'fixer', the specialist in cutting a way through the jungle of red tape which they have largely created.

The social and moral earnestness of the Soviet school is obviously not enough. As one specialist in this field put it, 'It is possible to work out what is right, to teach children what is right, and even to get them to understand *why* it is right. The problem lies in making sure that they *do* what is right.'[2] Also, ideals that are allowed to become orthodoxies can degenerate alarmingly. Soviet patriotism all too easily shades off into strident jingoism and xenophobia (with a touch of anti-Semitism too at times, for all the Constitution's outlawing of all kinds of racialism); and concern for the importance of the collective as a moral force can decline into mere social conformity, which leaves ample room for the prig and the time-server to flourish. These are international phenomena, not peculiar to the Soviet Union; but it is clear that an ethic of love of Motherland and Party and the struggle for the building of Communism is no more successful as a moral panacea than religious dogma, the Frontier Spirit, or compulsory games and cold showers.

From the point of view of many British or American observers, the rigidity of the Soviet school system is daunting, with its tight central control and near-uniformity of curricula and even methods for practically every school in the country. Education, however, like politics, is the art of the possible. Considering the enormous difficulties facing the Soviet régime after the Revolution, it is extremely doubtful if gradualist or *laissez faire* policies could have achieved much, let alone brought the system to where it now stands. Even now, most of the defects in school organization seem to arise when local officials have not been putting central policies into effect (as with measures to improve the position of girls, for example), and intervention from the top is more likely than local initiative to put things right. Decentralization, especially on the American pattern, would inevitably lead to further discrepancies in the standards of schooling, and widen the gap between town and country in particular. Uniform curricula do have some advantages in a country where the population is becoming increasingly mobile, by enabling children to continue their schooling in a new area without loss of time or much need for readjustment. Prescribed methods of teaching help some teachers at least, as we have seen, while standard regulations for children's behaviour mean that teachers and pupils alike know at least what is expected (though interpretations can, of course, vary).[3] In any case, central control is familiar enough in Western as well as Eastern European countries; a Frenchman or a Swede might well dislike the use made of central control in the Soviet Union, but would find the *fact* of centralization quite normal. Finally, it has to be recognized that though ultimate central control in the U.S.S.R. has abated not one whit, its exercise has become a little less rigid over the last decade. The introduction of optional courses in the ten-year school has meant a greater degree of pupil choice than was formerly possible. Even when the curricula for higher educational institutions are still centrally prescribed, the practice of leaving substantial amounts of curricular time to 'courses determined by the peculiarities of the Republic or the VUZ' is now common, and it is possible (as we have seen) for some institutions at least to design their own curricula, subject of course to central approval. Further, the incidence in the educational press of accounts of this 'interesting experiment' or that 'striking innovation in teaching' suggests that more flexibility enters the scene by stealth than would be approved at the outset; and now we find that the principle on 'individualized instruction' is becoming accepted in the schools.[4] The area for individual, local, or institutional discretion is still very small, but it is there, and has grown over the last decade, if only because the authorities are coming to recognize that the speed of change is too great for the cumbersome machinery of uniform change, and that a degree of flexibility need not, after all, be incompatible with keeping the hands of the central authorities on all essential matters.

On the other hand, substantial uniformity is still required, and there is little doubt that some Soviet teachers, especially the more imaginative, do feel some frustration. New ideas for school organization, lesson procedure, or almost anything else, are supposed to go through 'normal channels' – and these are liable to become clogged, particularly in a system as complex and all-embracing as that of the U.S.S.R. The government is in favour, in theory at least, of eventual devolution of more responsibility to local bodies in education as in other things (Lunacharski's stillborn plan for 'pedagogic Soviets' to run the schools, dropped in the 1920s, now gets the occasional friendly mention in discussion),[5] but the few moves in this direction have been small and hesitant. Some variations in practice do, as we have seen, exist with the blessing of the authorities (and a great many more without it), but as long as the conviction remains that there must be one 'correct' solution for every problem, uniformity is likely to remain the general rule, and its effects are just as likely to be stultifying as supportive.

One of the advantages of studying someone else's educational system is that it can stimulate us to take a closer and harder look at our own. This is not to suggest that we can or should lift educational ideas and practices out of context and transplant them into ours. Even closely similar societies can find that educational practices do not travel well, and it is clear that many aspects of Soviet education would be quite inappropriate to our own society. Nevertheless, we can still learn something from the U.S.S.R., and it may be that some of its ideas, suitably modified to our own different needs, might prove extremely useful. Among the issues in which Soviet experience can give us food for thought are the links between the school and other educational agencies, such as the family and the youth organizations; the place of science and technology, vocational and technical education; the attitude to streaming and selection in the schools; part-time education, especially at the higher levels; further education and in-service training and the place of women in education.

It is a commonplace almost everywhere that education, in the widest sense, goes on outside the school as well as in it, and one does not have to be a 'de-schooler'[6] to take the point that it is the out-of-school influences that can be the most powerful. Most educational systems take at least some account of this. The Soviet Union, however, pays rather more attention to these influences than do most other countries, with its deliberate control of the mass media such as the Press, television, the cinema, etc., the highly developed system of parent–teacher consultation, and the important part played in the whole process by the Pioneers and the Komsomol. Opinion in the West does not accept the idea of so much control of the mass media; the idea is not opposed in principle, as prosecutions for blasphemy, the banning of cigarette advertising on television, certain provisions of the Race Relations Act, and a host of other measures right back to the banning of 'horror comics' in 1955 make clear. It is irrelevant whether one approves of this particular list of prohibitions or not; acceptance of any of them (or others like them) means acceptance of the right of the State to control the expression of opinion to some degree in the public interest. Views differ as to what the public interest is, and how far control should be exercised, and with what safeguards; apart from some vocal and well-publicized

lobbies, few would care to go nearly as far as the Soviet authorities do. But the principle is widely conceded, even if we baulk at
the extent.

As for the work of the Parents' Committees, and the obligation
of the school to keep in touch with the pupils' homes, it is
obvious that this greatly helps the Soviet teacher. It is doubtful if
quite such a close connection is possible in our very different
social atmosphere, but it could fairly be asked if enough is done
in this country to acquaint parents with the work of the school
and the teachers with the parents' outlook and problems. With
the spread of full secondary education, parents are often called
upon to make decisions about their children's courses, while they
themselves may lack the information necessary to understand
what is happening in the school. Some schools, of course, have
always done a great deal to keep contact with the children's
families by means of parent–teacher associations, school open
days, consultation with individual parents, information leaflets,
and so on. There is also a growing awareness of the importance
of parental participation at a political level; it is early days yet,
but the development of Schools Councils in Scotland and the
recommendations of the Taylor Report in England, and the
modest growth of Community Schools in both countries, may
point to large-scale parental involvement as a matter of policy.
But the general picture is still uneven; all too often, the only time
teachers and parents come together is an occasional meeting
where mutual regard is expressed, with visits from parents (in-
dividually or in categories) to inquire about their children's
chances in the examination stakes. Many parents point out,
quite justly, that the best-organized parent–teacher bodies involve too much preaching to the converted; the very parents who
most need consultation with the school are the ones who can
rarely be induced to have anything to do with it, unless it is to
complain about some disciplinary matter. The social pressures
which work on the recalcitrant Soviet parent are not available
here, and it is doubtful if there is any other inducement that could
be as effective. The bait of examination passes is all very well for
those whose children can come within at least hoping distance of

success, but this does not solve the problem of 'selling' education to the rest. For all the moderately encouraging developments of the last few years, a great deal still remains to be done.

Again, there is no likelihood of a unified youth movement of the Soviet type operating here, but its use as an integral part of the educational system merits some attention. The present British youth organizations can, on the whole, provide a useful contribution to the social, moral, recreational, and physical education of their members. Their functions, essentially, are not all that different from those of the Pioneers and Komsomol; the most obvious difference is that most young people in this country never come near the youth organizations. The Soviet school takes account of the youth movement's work in its own, while few of our schools do, even where there is a big enough proportion of membership to justify it. The Soviet organizations are heavily subsidized and provided with trained youth leaders, while ours are usually short of leaders and suffer from a chronic and crippling shortage of money; government spending on the youth service is so small that those trying to make it work regard it as the Cinderella of the educational system. (It has to compete for this unenviable title, however, with educational research and adult education, of which more presently.) As with the problems of family–school relations, the absence of a favourable social atmosphere rules out any easy solutions. Nevertheless, the Soviet authorities have managed to make the youth organizations into an immensely valuable ally of the teachers, in school and out; there is little evidence that we are even contemplating anything of the kind. On the contrary, when the economic winds blow cold, the ancillary services suffer worse than most, with little evidence of concern for the long-term educational implications.

Science and technology are heavily stressed at every stage of the Soviet educational system, as we have seen, both for practical and ideological reasons. To many in this country the emphasis may seem excessive, but it is worth considering how far we are prepared to go on being outdistanced. Certainly, the sciences have been improving their status in our schools over the past decade or two, and in some places at least technical education is no longer considered to be a second-best. Yet there is still a widespread assumption in our universities that applied studies, such as engineering, are somehow less worthy than the purely theoretical. In many of our schools, technical subjects are regarded as the preserve of pupils judged incapable of doing anything else. In spite of the fact that we are living in a technological age, a large proportion of our young people leave school with little idea of the fundamentals of science and even less of technical subjects; we still tend to equate 'technical' with 'vocational' and assume that future professional and white-collar workers have no need to know anything about machinery, tools, materials, or technical processes. The spirit of Plato and Aristotle, who dismissed technical knowledge and skill as 'unworthy', is far from dead. In the Soviet Union, however, the view is now taken that for the future citizen of an industrial society some familiarity with industrial production should be just as much part of his general education as theoretical science, language, or social studies, whether or not his job will involve him directly in work of this kind. This view is taken partly for political reasons that are not applicable here, but we too live in an industrial society, and we too, perhaps, could re-examine our idea of what a growing child should be taught about the world he lives in.

The question of 'streaming' or grading by innate ability is such a vexed one in our own educational system that the experience of other countries must inevitably claim our interest. At first glance, the prevalent attitudes in the two systems are worlds apart. Most teachers in this country assume that children have widely different degrees of inborn intelligence, which is affected only slightly by anything that can be done in the school; that the best approach is to divide children into groups according to their level of ability, teaching them within the limits of their predetermined capacity, and that some method of intelligence testing can best show what these limits are. The Soviet view, on the other hand, is that environment is much more important than heredity in determining ability; that children should be graded only by age and attainment, not some supposed level of innate intelligence; that the teacher's aim should be to bring them all up to the required level; and that such devices as intelligence tests, by undervaluing the contribution of learning, limit the child's chances from the start and therefore must not be used. The available evidence suggests that both these points of view are overstated, as many teachers in both countries are coming to suspect. In the Soviet schools, the insistence on teaching children of practically all levels together must raise many difficulties for teachers and pupils alike. At whatever level the teacher pitches his lessons, there are always some who cannot keep up and some who will be held back. To suggest that children are not naturally bright or dull, but only well or badly taught, does not square with the facts of any system, Soviet or other, and indeed such a stark statement of the position is seldom heard nowadays. To have the quick children help the slower is undoubtedly of some use, but it has its limitations, as many teachers are aware; recent moves in the direction of 'individualized instruction' can be seen as an attempt to allow for these differences while avoiding the politically unacceptable solution of streaming.

Many of our schools, however, are just as uncritical in their acceptance of the doctrine of predetermined intelligence as the Soviet schools are in their rejection of it. There seems to be little agreement among our psychologists about the definition of intelligence. Also, there is far too much blind faith in the apparently precise Intelligence Quotient rating obtained from standardized tests. This is a complicated and controversial subject, and space does not permit even an outline of the major issues here.[7] Suffice to say that I.Q. is a more meaningful concept than Soviet psychologists allow, but only as a rough rule-of-thumb; the attempts of some British and American psychologists to prove that it is finely accurate are not altogether convincing. The value of intelligence tests in predicting performance in secondary schools, for example, is higher than any other known method, but there is still an estimated error of five or ten per cent. Such prophecies tend to be self-fulfilling in any case; a child assigned at eleven to a secondary modern course is likely to settle at that level, even if his potential is in fact higher; the later performances of 'failed-eleven-plus' children in some comprehensive schools have often borne this out. Again, if a child's I.Q. is as mathematically accurate as is sometimes believed, his performance on later tests should be exactly the same. In fact, it is usually quite close, but not close enough to be certain in the large number of borderline cases. In short, we tend to accept the idea of predetermined intelligence a little too readily. The numerical formulae involved in tests give them an appearance of precision they do not possess. The experience of the Soviet schools does not justify our throwing the whole idea of innate intelligence overboard, but they do seem to get good results with what most of our schools would regard as unpromising material. Perhaps if we used our schools less as a selective net for the academic we might find that we have been too timid in our assessment of what is possible.

Part-time education, especially at the higher level, is still an important aspect of the Soviet system. For those undergoing it, this has the disadvantage of making the courses longer and much more arduous, which is the main reason for reducing the proportion of students taking their qualifications in this way; nevertheless, a large proportion of the trained manpower of the U.S.S.R. is still obtained through the part-time system, and it means that the door to higher education need not be quite closed. Many people who would have been denied such opportunities in an entirely full-time system can pursue their studies in the evenings or by correspondence, to their own benefit and that of the community at large. This is a field where Britain is lagging far behind. There are exceptions, of course, notably the Open University, which has not only broken new ground in the provision of part-time courses, but has pioneered appropriate teaching methods and construction of courses; it has also been able to influence some of the existing institutions of higher education – St Andrews University made an agreement with the Open University for mutual recognition of courses in 1978, thus bringing into the university sector a practice that was already well established in some colleges of education. There is also a greater willingness in the universities to tolerate part-time study for post-graduate degrees, and in a few instances – a very few – this is possible at undergraduate level as well. But many of our institutions of higher education still regard any kind of external study with suspicion, and some even reject outright the idea that it can be worthy of the name of higher education. This is a doubly short-sighted view. It limits opportunities and wastes potential by setting so much store by performance (or inclination) at eighteen; and it is also against the interests of the institutions themselves. Until a few years ago, the problem was one of trying to find room for the growing numbers of young people seeking entry to universities and colleges. This is still true in some fields, but the problem now facing the higher institutions (and likely to face them well into the future, if current population forecasts are correct) is one of shrinking numbers as the birth-rate falls. Concentrating almost exclusively on full-time school leavers is not going to provide sufficient numbers; and unless the institutions are prepared to alter radically their requirements for admission (and they show little sign of doing this) they will either have to contract or develop some alternative clientele.[8] Part-time students, especially older ones, offer one such market – and the demand is there, judging from the numbers that apply for Open University courses, even now that the fees have been increased to the point where they are likely to deter all but the affluent or the very highly motivated. (It has to be remembered that full-time undergraduate students, even those on the mini-mum grant, have their fees paid; part-time students, with no grant, also have to find the now substantial sums to pay their fees themselves. To him that hath shall be given, and from him that hath not shall be taken away. It is ironic that at a time when more of our institutions are at last looking more favourably on part-time courses, for whatever reason, government-determined financial policies are making it more difficult to take up any opportunities that are created.)

The education of adults, whether for leisure and general culture or for further training and re-training for jobs, is the largest and fastest-growing sector of the Soviet educational system. As we have seen, periodic in-service training is a normal part of every teacher's career, and this applies to most other professions as well. Industry too plays its part; not all factories have adequate training facilities for instruction (this was one reason why the ambitious schemes for universal work practice by secondary school pupils often turned out to be unsatisfactory), but a great many have, and it is here, or in local centres, that workers can acquire higher levels of skill and thus improve both their work and their prospects; and since the pace of technological change can render skills obsolete, there are also facilities for re-training. This fits in with the growing tendency to expand general and polytechnical education and postpone vocational training more and more to the post-secondary stage. There is not much point in basing an adolescent's whole upper secondary schooling on specific training for a job that might not exist in ten or twenty years' time; but, given the likelihood of change, it does make sense to try to equip him with general and fundamental technical knowledge and concepts, and top that up with the specific job preparation. The last element, having a stronger foundation, can then be repeated at need throughout working life. There are also facilities for non-vocational education at all levels from the most elementary to the advanced, and there is even a network of political schools in which the Communist Party trains its personnel in Marxist–Leninist theory, techniques of administration and 'agitation' (i.e., explaining and justifying Party policies); these too operate at all levels, from the elementary evening classes in *politshkoly* (political schools) for rank and file members to the 'Party universities' for those on their way to higher posts in the Party *apparat*.[9] Whether one is thinking of personal cultivation, professional and vocational re-training, or of political activity, the point has obviously been taken that any form of education has to be a life-long process. In the early 1970s the number of people taking courses of this kind was approaching the twenty-million mark; by 1978 it was coming close to thirty-five millions.

It would be unfair to say that this area has been totally ignored in Britain. The Industrial Training Act has at least laid the basis for re-training and further development of skills, and the last few years have seen the appearance of two major reports on adult education, the Russell Report in England and Wales and the Alexander Report in Scotland.[10] It would be pleasant to be able to argue that these and similar developments have transformed the scene, but so far there is much more evidence of discussion than of action; adult education (or community or recurrent or lifelong education, or whatever of the many current terms we care to use) has become rather fashionable, partly because something is clearly amiss with the conventional system, and partly because our Continental neighbours, of whom we are slightly more aware these days, are nearly all far ahead of us in this respect. But actual results have so far been extremely disappointing. Little has been done to implement the two reports, and even existing facilities have been severely cut back in the name of economy; adult and recurrent education remain Cinderellas of the educational system. There is still a widespread tendency to dismiss this whole area as one of the 'frills' that can be safely trimmed whenever things become difficult. It is not entirely fair to blame local authorities for this; when they are required to cut back on educational spending, there is not a great deal that can be cut, since the bulk of what they do is required of them by law. Thus, adult education, teachers' in-service courses, recreational education – almost anything outside the mainstream of the formal system – becomes too easily the obvious victim for economies. This would not matter so much if we were sure what young people would need to know in twenty or thirty years' time, if we were sure that we were meeting their needs adequately through the present system, or if we could be reasonably certain that we were equipping them with the skills needed to educate themselves later in life as new and unforeseen needs arise. But we do none of these things. Now, it is perhaps too easy to blame the schools for their failure to provide anything that a large proportion of young people find remotely relevant to their needs and interests; interests change, and needs can arise from conditions that we cannot possibly foresee. Yet we put nearly all our resources into the education of children and young people through the formal school system, with a derisory provision for any kind of learning thereafter; we still adhere to the notion that education is essentially something that happens to children in schools; which, given the pace of social and technological change, is a recipe for obsolescence. If education is to keep pace with changing needs, we would do well to pay some attention to countries where more resources are given to continuing education; the U.S.S.R. is one of these.

The question of co-education may also be worth looking at. In Scotland at least it has never been a burning issue – most of the few single-sex schools have adopted segregation not from any educational consideration, but because they believe that it mirrors English practice and thus raises the 'social tone'. In England (and, for that matter, in France and Germany too) the issue is still a live one, and has given rise to much comment and speculation, accompanied by an almost complete absence of investigation. Broadly, the main argument for co-education is that it is the best way of avoiding the development of sexual repression,[11] but since there have been no controlled follow-up inquiries, and since there are so many other factors in determining sexual attitudes, there is little evidence that could be called conclusive. Opponents often argue that co-education, on the contrary, exposes the children to distraction and even moral[12] danger, but there is no evidence[13] to support this at all. It is true that girls, on average, mature faster than boys; but there is such a big overlap, and the developmental rates of individuals are so different, that this does not prove much either. The experiences of Scotland, Scandinavia, and the Soviet Union in this matter do not suggest that the mixing of the sexes does any harm. Nor, in fairness, do they support the notion that it can act as a psychological cure-all.

The place of women in the Soviet system merits rather more attention. Of students in higher education, about half are women. Three-quarters of the doctors, and a quarter of the engineers, are women. Women are as eligible for promoted posts as men; the men still predominate at the higher levels, but not to the same extent as is found here. There are no senior posts (headships of schools, for example) specifically reserved for men, nor do the universities and colleges have quotas for women entrants – both practices being common in this country until recently; and although the Sex Discrimination Act has now outlawed such practices, evidence of the survival of the attitudes that go with them be met daily. That a woman must choose between marriage and a career is less common in Britain than it was; in the U.S.S.R. the question is not permitted to arise. In theory, we have few specific bars left against women in higher education, but as a group they are still under a disadvantage. There are few places for them, they contribute only a minority of trained personnel, and there is still a widespread attitude that further education is somehow wasted on them. We have to ask ourselves if we can still afford even the remnants of masculine exclusiveness – unless, of course, we believe that women are, as a group, intellectually inferior to men, a belief that still survives but owes more to wishful thinking than to the available evidence.[14] Faced with international competition and ever-growing demands on our educational system, we need all the highly qualified people we can get, whatever their sex.

There are many aspects of Soviet education that are unlikely to commend themselves to the British observer. In teaching methods, for instance, it has little to offer in the way of constructive ideas. It is clear, too, that the achievements of the system are not always as great as the authorities claim, as can be seen from the continuous stream of complaints in *Uchitel'skaya gazeta* and elsewhere.[15] To anyone who rejects Marxist principles or communist policy (by no means necessarily the same thing), the basic aims of Soviet education will be unacceptable. In spite of its many failings, however, the system has made great strides since 1917, notably the virtual wiping out of illiteracy, the provision of a system of free, compulsory mass education in an erstwhile backward country, the spread of higher education, and the spectacular advance in many fields of science and technology. The lasting impression is that the U.S.S.R. cares about education, recognizes its importance as an instrument for securing the eventual well-being of society, and places it high on the list of national priorities. As Professor George Kline of Columbia University put it in 1958:

Conclusions and Comments

It is doubtful that any society has ever poured such a high proportion of its energies and resources into educational activities, in the broadest sense of the term, as the Soviet Union is doing today. Soviet leaders, from the beginning, have treated organized education with greater seriousness than political leaders in any other country, and this seriousness is widely shared by Soviet students and teachers, at every level of the school system.

This has taken a long time to be appreciated in the West. As another American, Dr Lawrence Derthick, U.S. Commissioner of Education, said about the same time:

We were simply not prepared for the degree to which the U.S.S.R. as a nation is committed to education as a means of national advancement . . . Our major reaction therefore is one of astonishment – and I choose the word advisedly – at the extent to which this seems to have been accomplished.

Such statements, from men who can hardly be said to be anxious to find complimentary things to say about the U.S.S.R., provide the biggest thinking-point of all. We still tend to think of education as a matter of personal benefit rather than national survival; we still too often assume that by educating individual X we are doing him a personal favour, as though he were the sole gainer in the process. Many of us, if we are frank about it, are still inclined to think of education as a luxury or a privilege. Faced with the challenge of the Soviet school, we have to consider whether we are giving education the attention, money, and effort that it deserves and demands. Words are cheap, and complacency is always dangerous even when justified. It is true that many features of our educational system yield nothing to that of the U.S.S.R., and that the Soviet system has many defects, some serious. But this kind of comparison is not very profitable. The main point is this: in the Soviet Union, education is regarded as a matter of first-rate national importance, and treated accordingly. Can we in Britain, in all honesty, say as much?

Notes

1. Introduction: The Background to the System

1. Although the 1959 Census lists over 100 nationalities, their numbers vary greatly. Over half of them have under 100,000 members, and about a quarter under 10,000. Variable, too, is their level of cultural development; among the non-Slav peoples, the Georgians and Armenians are outstanding in their possession of ancient and well-established native cultures. At the other extreme are the small tribal groups in the Arctic areas, with native cultures so primitive that they have to lean heavily on Russian models and methods for future development. The Central Asian peoples, such as the Tadzhiks, Kazakhs, Uzbeks, and Kirgiz, come between the two extremes.

2. Some sources state that newspapers are published in 119 different languages, but the official directory for 1955–60 lists only sixty-five. The extra fifty-four are probably not for internal consumption, but published in non-Soviet languages for export.

3. There are altogether five scripts in use: (1) the Cyrillic alphabet, which is used for Russian and the other Slavonic languages and, with modifications, for the great majority of the other languages as well, major and minor; (2) the Latin alphabet, used for Lithuanian, Latvian, and Estonian; (3) and (4) Georgian and Armenian have their own scripts; (5) the Hebrew alphabet, also used to write Yiddish.

4. For an official exposition of the language issue, see: M. I. Isayev, *National Languages in the U.S.S.R.: Problems and Solutions*, (Progress Publishers, Moscow, 1977).

5. *Constitution (Fundamental Law) of the Union of Soviet Socialist Republics*, (Novosti Press Agency Publishing House, Moscow, 1977).

6. The figures for literacy and school provision in the non-Russian areas are derived from Soviet sources (see, for example, Korolev: *Education in the U.S.S.R.*, pp. 70–76). Some caution is called for on two points:

(1) It is possible that the numbers of schools refer only to European

Notes

schools of the colonial type and do not include Muslim schools, for which no figures are available.

(2) It has been suggested that the literacy figures were derived from the writings of Russians before 1914 who were seeking to justify the annexation of these territories by stressing the backwardness of their peoples. They may therefore be underestimates.

Even allowing for some exaggeration, however, the recan be no doubt of the general educational backwardness of these areas before the First World War.

7. 1926 Census. Literacy for the entire country was given as 51 per cent. The republic with the highest level was the Ukraine, with 57·5 per cent; the lowest was Tadzhikistan, with 3·7 per cent.

8. The following table shows the numerical growth of the system between 1914 and 1977:

	1914/ 15	1940/ 41	1965/ 66	1970/ 71	1975/ 76	1976/ 77
Total studying: (thousands) of whom:	10,588	47,547	71,857	79,634	92,605	93,708
in general educational schools	9,656	35,552	48,255	49,193	47,594	46,468
in vocational-technical schools	106	717	1,701	2,591	3,381	3,552
in secondary specialized schools	54	975	3,659	4,388	4,525	4,623
in higher education institutions	127	812	3,861	4,581	4,854	4,950
in adult and further education	645	9,491	14,381	18,881	32,251	34,115

Source: *Narodnoe khozyaistvo SSSR 1917–1977: Statisticheskii ezhegodnik* p. 575, (Moscow, 1977).

9. *Strengthening the Ties of the School with Life, and Further Developing the System of Public Education.* Theses of the Central Committee of the Communist Party of the Soviet Union and the U.S.S.R. Council of Ministers, November 1958, Section 20. (Published in English as *Bringing the Soviet Schools Still Closer to Life*, Soviet Booklet No. 44, London 1958.)

10. Osnovy zakonodatel'stva Soiuza SSR i soiuznykh respublik o narodnom obrazovanii. (Basic Law of 19 July 1973, text in *Uchitel'skaya*

gazeta 5 April 1973. For an analysis and commentary in English, see Seymour Rosen, *Education in the U.S.S.R.: Recent Legislation and Statistics*, U.S. Department of Health, Education and Welfare, Washington D.C., 1975.)

11. The course of lessons on the Constitution of the U.S.S.R. was replaced in January 1963 by a new course of 'Social Study' (*Obshchestvovedenie*). The textbook for the course is divided into five sections (1) 'Elementary Marxism–Leninism', an account of the philosophical bases of communist doctrine; (2) 'Socialism', an outline of the theory of Soviet government and law; (3) 'The Communist Party', dealing with the Party's organization and role; (4) 'From Socialism to Communism', an outline of the aims and problems of the 1961 Party programme; (5) 'The Twentieth Century – the Century of the Triumph of Communism', a survey of world revolutionary and anti-colonial movements. The general emphasis of the course is on putting Party policy in its theoretical setting in terms that can be readily grasped by seventeen-year-old pupils.

The latest syllabus was issued in 1975. (*Obshchestvovedenie: Programma dlya srednei obshcheobrazovatel'noi shkoly i srednikh spetsial'nykh uchebnykh zavedenii*, Politizdat, Moscow, 1975. The programme is issued jointly by the Ministry of Education of the U.S.S.R. and the Ministry of Higher and Secondary Specialized Education of the U.S.S.R.)

12. e.g. *Nasha rodina: Geograficheskii atlas dlya 4-go klassa srednei shkoly*, (Moscow 1965 + revisions). For observations, see Bereday, Brickman and Read, *The Changing Soviet School*, p. 13.

2. The Educational System: General Characteristics (Part One)

1. English now has an overwhelming lead.

2. 'Sel'skii Uchitel' – Problemy, Suzhdeniya.' *Uchitel'skaya gazeta*, 25 May 1967.

3. The following table shows the general trends in enrolment of women students between 1940 and 1977.

	1940/41	1965/66	1970/71	1975/76	1976/77
% of women in higher education (total)	58	44	49	50	51
% of women students in engineering	40	31	38	40	40
agriculture	46	26	30	33	33

	1940/41	1965/66	1970/71	1975/76	1976/77
economics and law	64	54	60	62	63
medicine and PE	74	54	56	56	57
education and art	66	66	66	68	68
% of women in sec. spec. education (total)	55	50	54	54	55
% of women students in engineering	32	35	40	41	41
agriculture	37	36	37	37	37
economics and law	60	80	83	85	85
medicine and PE	83	87	87	88	89
education and art	60	81	81	82	83

Source: *Narodnoe khozyaistvo SSSR 1917–1977*, p. 596.

4. Ludwig Liegle, *Familienerziehung und sozialer Wandel in der UdSSR*, (Quelle und Meyer, Heidelberg; Ost Europa-Institut an der Frein Universität Berlin, 1970).

5. *Komunist Tadzhikistana*, 8 June 1973; *Turkmenskaya iskra*, 2 February 1972; *Pravda Vostoka*, 24 February 1970; *Uchitel'skaya gazeta*, 27 January 1973. For fuller treatment see: N. Grant, 'Sexual Equality in the Communist World', *Compare* Vol. IV, No. 1, Jan. 1974, pp. 24–30.

6. D. Balaev, 'Vtorogodnichestvo preodolevaetsya'. *Narodnoe obrazovanie*, No. 2, 1965, pp. 13–14.

7. I am indebted for information and interpretation in this section to Mrs Marion Blythman, Principal Lecturer in Special Education, Moray House College of Education, Edinburgh, after a visit in 1978.

8. This is based on conversations with teachers in Moscow and Leningrad, 1962, Moscow and Minsk, 1968, and Moscow, Kiev, and Erevan, 1976.

3. *The Educational System: General Characteristics (Part Two)*

1. *Sovietskaya pedagogika*, October 1943. The 'Rules for Pupils' were adopted in August 1943 and have been in force ever since. Every pupil has them on his individual school identity card. The 'Moral Code of the Builder of Communism' (*Moral'nyi kodeks stroitel'ya kommunizma*) is normally displayed prominently in the school hall.

2. This scheme is a draft programme prepared by the Bureau of Moral Education of the Institute of History and Theory of Pedagogy of the Academy of Pedagogic Sciences of the R.S.F.S.R. It is more fully dealt with in Bereday, Brickman, and Read, *The Changing Soviet*

School, pp. 427–37. For an excellent account of the whole process of socialization, see Urie Bronfenbrenner, *Two Worlds of Childhood: U.S.A. and U.S.S.R.*

3. The All-Union Lenin Pioneer Organization (*Vsesoyuznaya Pionerskaya Organizatsiya imeni V. I. Lenina*) is officially described as 'a mass children's organization which brings up children in the spirit of love and devotion to the Motherland, friendship between nations and proletarian internationalism; it draws Pioneers and schoolchildren into public life, develops in them a conscientious attitude towards study discipline, love of work, and curiosity; it brings up children to be all-round, developed individuals, conscientious, healthy, courageous, full of the joy of life, and unafraid of difficulties, future builders of Communism'. (*Bolshaya Sovietskaya Entsiklopediya*, 1955).

4. Strictly speaking, many of the out-of-school institutions mentioned here are not run directly by the Pioneer Organization. The Young Naturalists' Stations, for example, are directed by the Central Station for Young Naturalists, and the Children's Technical Stations by a similar central body; many facilities provided by the Pioneers, such as holiday camps, are duplicated by others run by trade unions and similar bodies. The Ministries of Education and Culture, in particular, are responsible for a variety of services, such as the Children's Theatres. This spreading of responsibility, however, makes little difference in practice; the entire network of recreational education in the U.S.S.R. is so closely bound up with the work of the Pioneer Organization that it seems appropriate to deal with all the children's institutions in this section. Clubs and circles for older pupils, students in higher education, and young workers, are coordinated in much the same way by the Komsomol.

5. The word *druzhina* does not mean a brigade in the military sense (*brigada*); it is connected with the word for 'friend', and is often used to describe various kinds of voluntary groups, such as Workers' Brigades, armed or otherwise. Its connotations are militant without being military.

6. There is a high turnover rate among professional youth leaders. One reason is that many of them do the job for a couple of years or so after finishing a Secondary Specialized School, then go on to take a full teacher's training course.

7. The word 'Komsomol' is, of course, a compound of the initial syllables of the last three words. This is typical of the Soviet habit of giving things extremely unwieldy titles, then reducing them to manageable size by running together lopped-off bits of the key words.

197

Such terms have added considerably to the Russian vocabulary since 1917.

8. Over eighty per cent of all students are Komsomol members, at least nominally. (*Partiinaya zhizn'* No. 1, January 1958).

9. Membership also necessarily means a surrender of some personal freedom. For example, a youth may go to church if he wishes, but a Komsomol who does so is liable to be severely criticized or even expelled, since adherence to any religion is incompatible with the movement's principles. Some Komsomols do in fact go to church; that they are not expelled may be due to negligence or apathy in their branches, or to the hope that they will soon get over the habit. Membership of the Communist Party involves similar limitations, but there seems to be greater strictness in enforcing them.

10. *Resolyusii i Dokumenty XII Syezda VLKSM*. (Molodaya Gvardiya, Moscow, 1954.)

11. The three 'steps' are detailed in *Uchitel'skaya gazeta*, 31 July 1958. The first of them consists of the following requirements:

1. Know why we celebrate the great holidays – 23 February, 8 March, 22 April, 1 and 2 May, 9 May, 7 and 8 November, 5 December.
2. Learn the hymn of the U.S.S.R. and your Republic.
3. Know the meaning of the Red Banner, the Pioneer Scarf and Pin, the salute of the Young Pioneers.
4. Know the great deeds of the Pioneer Organization and its heroes.
5. Know the heroes after whom your brigade, detachment, school, and street are named, and local heroes.
6. Know the song of the Young Pioneers.
7. Make something necessary for school work, together with your 'link'.
8. Make something necessary for the Pioneer Room of your school, together with your 'link'.
9. Help your elders with the housework: set the table, wash the dishes, make something for your home.
10. Plant trees or flowers and care for them.
11. Care for useful birds, make bird-tables and bird-houses.
12. Learn to distinguish poisonous mushrooms and berries from edible ones.
13. Learn to take care of your person: sew on buttons, darn your socks, make your own bed, wash yourself and your underwear.

14. Do your morning physical exercises.
15. Learn how to run quickly, throw a ball accurately, jump, ski, swim, and balance on a plank.
16. Learn how to form a line-up, distinguish Pioneer signals on trumpet and drum, number off.
17. Learn three to five games of various kinds – table games, games of movement, etc.
18. Go on at least two one-day marches, know how to pack a rucksack, how to orient yourself by compass, how to make a fire and cook on it, etc.
19. Learn two or three Pioneer songs and mass dances with your comrades.

4. *The Schools*

1. A. V. Zaporozhets, L. E. Zhurova, T. V. Turantaeva, 'Psikhologopedagogicheskie problemy vozmozhnostei obucheniya i podgotovki k shkole detei doshkol'nogo vozrasta', *Sovietskaya pedagogika* 1975, No. 6, pp. 42–9. For a fuller discussion, see N. Grant, 'The U.S.S.R.', in Maurice Chazan (ed.), *International Research in Early Childhood Education*, pp. 195–210, (NFER Publishing Co., 1978).

2. As early as 1965, Anatoly Shustov, deputy Minister of Education of the R.S.F.S.R., was quoted as saying that nurseries and kindergartens had room for fifty-one per cent of the relevant age-group (*The Times Educational Supplement*, 2 April 1965). By the 1970s, the number of enrolments in the U.S.S.R. as a whole had risen to over ten million. This is still only thirty-three per cent of the entire age-group, but enrolment tends to be concentrated at the upper age-levels; thus, a substantial majority of older pre-school children having some experience of kindergarten is quite consistent with this general overall figure.

3. Transition from the primary to the secondary stage used to be after class IV. As the change-over to the present system took many years, it is quite probable that some schools in the more remote areas are still working on the old system.

4. In the U.S.S.R., as here, there are constant efforts to keep the size of classes down nearer the thirty mark; there, as here, the success of such attempts varies enormously from place to place.

5. The number of 'language schools' has more than doubled since the early 1960s.

6. Source: Akademiya pedagogicheskikh nauk RSFSR: *Obshchaya ob'yasnitel'naya zapiska k pererabotannym proektam uchebnogo plana i programm srednei shkoly*, pp. 9–10. (1965. Prosveshchenie, Moscow.)

7. The current syllabus in physical education also makes some provision for more choice and flexibility after the fifth form, but the basic programme is detailed throughout, stipulating not only the skills to be taught, but the methods to be used and the standards acceptable for children of any given age. Duplicated circular, 1978.

8. In some of the republics, the total school course is a year longer than in Russian schools. Lithuania, Latvia, and Estonia, for example, have been authorized to carry on with eleven-year schooling to accommodate the time needed for extra language teaching. (*Vedomosti Verkhovnogo Sovieta S S S R*, 19 August 1965.)

9. It is becoming increasingly common for the more ambitious parents in the non-Russian areas to opt to send their children to Russian-language schools, where considerably less time is spent on the vernacular than in the native-language schools; the better knowledge of Russian thus obtained will improve their chances of entering higher education elsewhere in the U.S.S.R. There is a good deal of controversy over this point; many observers see in the growth of the Russian-language schools an attempt to strengthen Russian at the expense of the other languages. This is the view taken by Yaroslav Belinsky in 'The Soviet Educational Laws of 1958–9 and Soviet Nationality Policy', *Soviet Studies*, Vol. 14, No. 2, October 1962. Although any such intention is vociferously denied by the authorities, fears of a covert policy of Russification are rarely far below the surface; in 1978, on the adoption of the new Constitution, the version for Georgia did not mention the Georgian language as *the* official language of the Republic. After riots, the change was made, but the worries remain, especially in republics with weaker native cultures than Georgia.

10. 'V Ts K K P S S i Sovete Ministrov S S S R. O merakh dal'neishego uluchsheniya raboty srednei obshcheobrazovatel'noi shkoly.' *Pravda*, 19 November 1966.

11. M. A. Prokofiev, 'Vuzy – shkole', *Vestnik vysshei shkoly*, No. 9, 1966, pp. 7–11. This has not yet happened, however.

12. The 1958 measures introduced two hours a week for optional studies in the final forms. This principle has been greatly extended under the latest scheme. (Akademiya pedagogicheskikh nauk R S F S R, *Obshchaya ob'yasnitel'naya zapiska k pererabotannym proektam uchebnogo plana i programm srednei shkoly*, pp. 26–31. (Prosveshchenie, Moscow, 1965.) Recent changes involve some reduction of time, as part of a general lightening of the weekly load.

13. Ibid., as modified by the Basic Law.

14. M. A. Prokofiev, op. cit.

15. Unlike the G.C.E., however, the 'Attestation of Maturity' has no differentiation of grades corresponding to the Ordinary and Advanced levels, nor is anything like the same degree of specialization possible. The German *Abitur* examinations would be a closer parallel.

16. Ministerstvo vysshego i srednego spetsial'nogo obrazovaniya S S S R, *Spravochnik dlya postupayushchikh v srednie spetsial'nye uchebnye zavedeniya S S S R (teckhnikumy, uchilischcha, shkoly) v 1966 godu* ('Vysshaya Shkola', Moscow, 1966.) *passim.*

17. Ibid., pp. 378–82, and *passim.*

18. 'Desyatiletnyaya, trudovaya, politekhnicheskaya', *Uchitel'skaya gazeta*, 15 August 1964.

19 Ibid.

20. M. A. Prokofiev, op. cit.

21. e.g., M. A. Prokofiev, 'Segodnya i zavtra nashei shkoly', *Pravda*, 12 December 1966; 'V devyatyi klass', *Uchitel'skaya gazeta*, 11 April 1967.

22. The position with regard to music schools is rather more complicated. There are thirteen music *desyatiletki* (ten-year schools) in Moscow, Leningrad, Kiev, Odessa, Tbilisi, Kharkov, Riga, Baku, Yerevan, Tashkent, Alma-Ata, Gorky, and Minsk. These schools are highly selective, and are affiliated to music conservatories, which ninety per cent of their pupils enter. There is also a much more widespread two-tier system: over 1,200 *vos'miletki* (eight-year schools), from which pupils go on to the appropriate *uchilishcha* (secondary schools). These offer a four-year course, which includes musical and educational theory. From there, students can either proceed to a conservatory or go into teaching.

23. 'Strengthening the ties of the school with life and further developing the system of public education.' Text of the memorandum by N. S. Khrushchov, approved by the Praesidium of the Central Committee of the Communist Party of the Soviet Union, in September 1958, p. 10. (Published in English as *Proposals to Reform Soviet Education*, Soviet Booklet No. 42, October 1958.)

24. For: Academician N. N. Semyonov, *Pravda*, 17 October 1958; I. Zeldovich and A. Sakharov, *Pravda*, 19 November 1958; V. Koruyedov, *Uchitel'skaya gazeta*, 9 October 1958, etc.

Against: Academician M. Lavrentiev, *Pravda*, 25 November 1958; I. Eichfeld, *Pravda*, 22 December 1958; P. Litvinenko, *Pravda*, 13 December 1958, etc.

Some of the principal arguments are paraphrased in Bereday, Brickman, and Read, *The Changing Soviet School*, pp. 374–8.

Notes

25. *The Times Educational Supplement*, 15 March 1963. This school has since been the subject of a documentary programme on British television.

26. 'Olympiads' are national competitions in academic subjects, chess, the fine arts, etc. They are not to be confused with major sports events ('Spartakiads').

27. This was the target set by the seven-year plan. There is some doubt, however, whether it was fully achieved, and the available figures are not clear enough for certainty. One estimate suggests one and a half million as a more likely figure for 1965. (Harold J. Noah, *Financing Soviet Schools*, pp. 37–8. Columbia University Press, 1966.)

28. 'Soviet Boarders: Home Every Sunday', *The Times Educational Supplement*, 22 October 1965.

29. Admittedly, 'upbringers' is a clumsy term for *vospitateli*, but it is the most accurate translation. Some American writers call them 'educators', but this invites confusion with ordinary teachers. The Scots term 'wean-herd' is neat, but unfortunately is not easily rendered into Southern English.

30. Harold J. Noah, op. cit., p. 108.

31. The five-year courses were exceptional; most of the vocational schools offered courses of two years and under.

32. The population in 1941 was about 200 millions, in 1945 between 170 and 175 millions. The loss of birth-rate must have been about ten millions – a total loss of thirty-five to forty millions.

33. N. S. Khrushchov, op. cit., p. 4.

34. N. S. Khrushchov, op. cit., p. 5.

35. V. Shubkin (articles in *Kommunist*, February 1966, and *Voprosy filosofii*, No. 5, 1966) caused something of a sensation by making it clear that there *is* a close correlation between socio-economic class and educational opportunity in the U.S.S.R. For a summary see Victor Zorza, 'Class Struggle Looming in Russia', the *Guardian*, 2 July 1966.

36. 'Desyatiletnyaya, trudovaya, politekhnicheskaya', *Uchitel'skaya gazeta*, 15 August 1964.

37. Ibid.

38. V. Ts K KPSS Soviete Ministrov SSSR 'Ob izmenenii sroka obucheniya v srednikh obshcheobrazovatel'nykh trudovykh politekhnicheskikh shkolakh s proizvodstvennym obucheniem'. *Sovietskaya Rossiya*, 13 August 1964.

39. 'Chto novogo v shkole?', *Sovietskaya Rossiya*, 25 August 1964.

40. 'Desyatiletnyaya, trudovaya, politekhnicheskaya', *Uchitel'skaya gazeta*, 15 August 1964.

41. The relevant section of the current plan (*Poryadok perekhoda na novyi uchebnyi plan, programmy i uchebniki*) sets out the following sequence for the introduction of the new curricula, schemes of work and textbooks:

School year 1967–68 – forms I and IV
School year 1968–69 – forms II, V, VI, and IX
School year 1969–70 – forms III, VII, VIII, and X

(Akademiya pedagogicheskikh nauk R S F S R, *Obschchaya ob'yasnitel'-naya zapiska k pererabotannym proektam uchebnogo plana i programm srednei shkoly*, p. 86. [Prosveshchenie, Moscow, 1965.])

42. Ibid., pp. 32–43.

43. There is no English equivalent. By this form of address, Irina Ivanovna Strakhova will be called 'Irina Ivanovna', which is more formal than 'Irina' but less so than 'Tovarishch Strakhova'. The Russian equivalents of 'Sir', etc. are no longer used.

44. P. Ya. Galperin and N. F. Talyzina, 'V osnove – upravlenie protsessom usvoeniya znanii', *Vestnik vysshei shkoly*, No. 6, 1965.

5. Higher Education

1. The number of institutions can fluctuate, owing to reorganization, while the number of students rises steadily. In 1960–61, for example, there were 739 institutions as against 880 in 1950–51; in the same decade the student population increased from about 1,356,000 to 2,395,000. (*Vysshee obrazovanie v S S S R: Statisticheskii sbornik*. Gosstatizdat, Moscow, 1961.)

2. *Narodnoe khozyaistvo S S S R 1917–1977: Statisticheskii yezhegodnik*, (Moscow, 1977).

3. Some use has been made of radio and television to help with correspondence courses, rather in the manner of the Open University but to a more limited extent. More use has been made of these methods over the last few years, but the complaint of V. I. Nyunka (*Vestnik vysshei shkoly*, No. 8, 1961) that the problem was being 'tinkered with' is still being reiterated, though with less force.

4. According to a study of the higher institutions in Sverdlovsk, the average drop-out rate for full-time students was 5·3 per cent per year, which meant that over a quarter of those admitted to a five-year course failed to graduate. (In some departments, notably natural science, forestry and agriculture, the figure was appreciably higher.) Part-time students, however, did much worse than this; those taking

evening courses were failing at the rate of 12·7 per cent per year, while those taking correspondence courses were even more vulnerable (14·3 per cent per year). (M. N. Rutkevich, *Vestnik vysshei shkoly* 7, 1965.) How typical the Sverdlovsk study is of the country as a whole is not certain, but it is perhaps significant that through all the fluctuations of the proportions of full- and part-time students, full-timers have consistently provided the majority of graduates (*Narodnoe khozyaistvo SSSR v 1969 godu*). Calls for improvement of part-time courses have certainly become widespread and persistent; a commonly made point is that courses should be more individualized and adapted to the students' needs and experience, not simply copies of the full-time programme (e.g., A. I. Bogomolov: 'Povyshat' kachestvo podgotovki zaochnikov i vechernikov', *Vestnik vysshei shkoly*, No. 8, 1969, pp. 3–8).

5. *Vestnik vysshei shkoly*, No. 4, 1961, pp. 6–7. The Statute (*Polozhenie o vysshikh uchebnykh zavedeniyakh SSSR*) replaces the 'Model Charter' (*Tipovoi ustav*) which had been in force since 1938. Its provisions were incorporated into the Basic Law of 1973.

6. Some disciplines, such as law and economics, are taught both in universities and special institutes.

7. The findings of a survey of the Novosibirsk region are dealt with fully by Murray Yanowitch and Norton Dodge, 'Social class and education: Soviet findings and reactions', *Comparative Education Review*, October 1968, XII, 3, pp. 248–67.

8. *Vestnik vysshei shkoly*, 1961, No. 8, pp. 50–52.

9. *Izvestiya*, 27 December 1960.

6. Teachers

1. *Narodnoe khozyaistvo SSSR 1917–1977*.

2. This is based largely on conversations in Moscow and Minsk in 1968, and in Moscow, Kiev, and Erevan in 1976.

3. *Postanovlenie TsK KPSS i SM SSSR*, 9 May 1963. See *The Times Educational Supplement*, 25 May 1963.

4. In areas where there is still a shortage of teachers, students on practice are sometimes simply given a timetable and told to get on with it. (This used to happen in Britain too, when teachers were in short supply.) One informant went so far as to say that whatever the programme for teaching practice said, there were many areas where it had been 'wiped out in practice' (*fakticheski likvidirovana*); he was echoing a phrase used in several articles during the 1960s, but ten years later (Moscow, 1976).

5. 'Teachers who have completed the university course do not love their profession, they take it up unwillingly, consider themselves as temporary sojourners in the pedagogic field, and at the very first opportunity gleefully quit the school.' (D. O. Lordkipanidze, 'Sozdat' pedagogicheskuyu atmosferu v universitetakh', *Sovietskaya pedagogika*, No. 5, 1965, pp. 100–104.

Some have been inclined to blame the universities rather than the students:

The whole history of university education in the U.S.S.R. testifies to an indissoluble link between the universities and the schools. One of the most important tasks of the universities has been and remains the training of highly qualified teachers. (But) in the pedagogic and upbringing work of the universities there are, unfortunately, many defects. Sometimes one hears that some teachers, graduates of the universities, are distinguished by weak training in the fields of pedagogy and teaching methods, insufficient knowledge of the secondary school syllabus in their subject, and unhelpfulness in fulfilling their functions as upbringers, class leaders, organizers of circles, etc. It has also happened that university students regard teaching with contempt, and avoid it in every possible way.

(I.S. Dubinina and I. M. Slepenkov, 'Universitet – uchitel' – shkola', *Vestnik vysshei shkoly*, No. 3, 1965, pp. 15–18.)

6. From the Director of the Moscow City Institute for Teacher Improvement, Moscow, 1976. Courses are detailed in *O sisteme perepodgotovki pedagogicheskikh kadrov g. Moskvy na 1975–1976 uchebnyi god* (*Prikaz Glavnogo upravleniya narodnogo obrazovaniya Mosgorispolkoma No. 172 ot 21 iyulya 1975 g*).

7. Conversations in Krupskaya Pedagogic Institute of Foreign Languages, Moscow, 1976.

8. 'Deistvovat' edinnym frontom', *Uchitel'skaya gazeta*, 3 July 1965.

9. The reason for making so much of this case may well go beyond questions of school organization and staff regulations. Stalin described Mayakovsky as the outstanding Soviet poet, and that was how he had to be presented in the school. As often happens, many teachers kept to the set line long after Stalin's death. The case of the pupil's essay was probably used as a means of letting teachers know that the former line on Mayakovsky was no longer required.

(The original article appeared in *Uchitel'skaya gazeta*, 22 November 1962. In the issue of 10 January 1963 it was stated that many letters had been received, and one on each side was published.)

10. Only a few secondary teachers or directors have higher degrees, though such titles as 'Honoured Teacher' may be found at all levels.

Notes

11. 'We must keep clearly in mind that curriculum and syllabus provide only the starting-point (in the development of the educational system). How it will work out depends wholly and utterly on the teacher – his cultural and scientific outlook, his specialist and pedagogic training, his pedagogic skill and devotion to the task of the communist upbringing of the rising generation. "As is the teachers, so is the school." This truth maintains its significance in our time too.'

(Akademiya pedagogicheskikh nauk R.S.F.S.R.: *Obschchaya ob'-yasnitel'naya zapiska k pererabotannym proektam uchebnogo plana i programm srednei shkoly*, p. 85. Prosveshchenie, Moscow, 1965.)

12. Textbook writing can be extremely lucrative. The royalties from one book used throughout the country have been known to total as much as an ordinary teacher's earnings for his entire professional career.

13. George S. Counts, 'A Word about the Soviet Teacher' (*Comparative Education Review*, Vol. 5, No. 1, June 1961).

7. Conclusion and Comments

1. Sidney and Beatrice Webb, *Soviet Communism: a New Civilization*.

2. Oral communications, Moscow 1976.

3. Bronfenbrenner, op. cit. An illustration of a poster making the point that a Pioneer 'always tells the truth and protects the honour of his detachment' shows a boy denouncing another in class.

4. Based largely on conversations in the Moscow Institute for Teacher Improvement and the Institute of Pedagogy of the Academy of Sciences of the Ukrainian S.S.R., Kiev, 1976.

5. See Sheila Fitzpatrick, *The Commissariat of Enlightenment: Soviet Organization of Education and the Arts under Lunacharsky*, (Cambridge University Press, 1970).

6. See Ivan Illich, *De-Schooling Society*, Penguin Books, 1973.

7. Intelligence testing is discussed heatedly and at length in a wide range of books and publications. A prominent supporter of the practice is H. J. Eysenck (*Uses and Abuses of Psychology* and *Know Your Own I.Q.*, both Pelicans); forceful opponents include Robin Pedley (*The Comprehensive School*, Pelican, 1963; rev. ed. 1978) and Brian Simon (*Intelligence Testing and the Comprehensive School*, Lawrence and Wishart, 1953). For a layman's guide to the use of testing to mystify rather than illuminate, see R. E. Bell and N. Grant, *A Mythology of British Education*, (Panther, 1974).

8. Department of Education and Science and the Scottish Education

Department, *Higher Education into the 1990s: A Discussion Document*, (London and Edinburgh, February 1978).

9. Ellen Mickiewicz, *Soviet Political Schools: The Communist Party Adult Instruction System*, (Yale University Press, New Haven and London, 1967).

10. e.g., Scottish Education Department: *Adult Education: The Challenge of Change*, (HMSO, Edinburgh, 1975). See also: Edgar Faure et al., *Learning to Be*, (UNESCO, Paris, 1972; UNESCO, *The School and Continuing Education: Four Studies*).

11. A. S. Neill, *That Dreadful School* (*passim*), and elsewhere. Neill is thought-provoking, but is generally regarded as an extremist.

12. Pope Pius XI in his Encyclical *Divini Illius Magistri* objected strongly to this 'promiscuous herding together of males and females on an equal footing', but many Catholics reject his point of view.

13. Surveys of the *opinions* of teachers and heads of schools seem to be the nearest thing we have approaching evidence on the topic of co-education. On few educational subjects can there have been so many pronouncements on the basis of so little evidence.

14. It might be thought that the principle of sex equality was now so widely accepted (and enshrined in law) that none of this should need saying, but the survival of idiot jokes about bra-burning makes one wonder – to say nothing of the ample evidence of more subtle kinds of discrimination. The works of Greer and others of the more militant camp are too well known to need mention here, but it might be useful to consider that some of the grosser delusions were effectively collapsed long ago. The intellectual capacity of the sexes is dealt with by Anthony Barnett, *The Human Species*, Chapter 10 (Pelican, 1957). (He also examines the concept of intelligence in the previous chapter.) Some of the most cherished myths about sex differences (and many other things) are entertainingly demolished by Bergen Evans in *The Natural History of Nonsense* (Michael Joseph, 1947).

15. One of the hazards of investigating Soviet education through Soviet sources is that one can all too easily make a collection of complaints and shortcomings, without knowing how representative they are. Relying too heavily on them can give just as distorted a picture as can the exclusive use of other Soviet sources, which insist that everything in the garden is lovely.

Select Bibliography

Ablin, Fred (ed.), *Contemporary Soviet Education* (1969, International Arts and Sciences Press, New York).
A useful collection of translated extracts from the Soviet press, with an introduction to clarify the context.

Alston, Patrick, *Education and the State in Tsarist Russia* (1969, Stanford University Press).
A clear and well-documented account of developments in Russian education up to the Revolution.

Bereday, George Z. F., Brickman, William W., and Read, Gerald H., eds., *The Changing Soviet School* (1960, Constable, London).
The (American) Comparative Education Society's field study in the U.S.S.R. Fairly lengthy and detailed, it contains a general survey of the Soviet educational system as well as chapters dealing with particular aspects, such as moral education, education out of school, polytechnical education, etc. There are many illuminating anecdotes to illustrate the more general points. Bias, where present, is usually obvious enough.

Bereday, George Z. F., and Pennar, Jaan, eds., *The Politics of Soviet Education* (1960, Stevens & Sons, London).
In spite of the title, this collection of essays considers several aspects of Soviet education as well as the directly political. Among the topics treated are the teaching of history, teacher training, anti-religious education, Moscow University, the youth movement, class tensions in education, etc. The contributions are amply documented, but some rely heavily on 'complaint-collecting'.

Bowen, James, *Soviet Education: Anton Makarenko and the Years of Experiment* (1965, University of Wisconsin Press, Madison).
An account of the life and ideas of the Soviet Union's most influential educational theorist.

Select Bibliography

Bronfenbrenner, Urie, *Two Worlds of Childhood: U.S.S.R. and U.S.A.*, (Simon and Schuster, New York, 1972).

A vivid, readable, and penetrating study of the socialization of children in the two countries.

Counts, George A., *The Challenge of Soviet Education* (1957, McGraw-Hill).

A full survey by an American observer of the Soviet school system viewed as a weapon of communist policy. It is now out of date in many respects, and should be approached with caution.

De Witt, Nicholas, *Education and Professional Employment in the U.S.S.R.* (1961, National Science Foundation, Washington).

Though mainly concerned with professional and vocational education, this book of 856 pages covers the entire system. Encyclopedically thorough, it is a mine of information for the serious student. Although very dated, it is still invaluable as a classic case-study.

Fitzpatrick, Sheila, *The Commissariat of Enlightenment: Soviet Organization of Education and the Arts under Lunacharsky* (1970, Cambridge University Press).

A readable and valuable account of the immediate post-revolutionary period; it is particularly useful in making clear many of the differences between that stage and the Stalin era that followed.

Hans, Nicholas, *The Russian Tradition in Education* (1963, Routledge & Kegan Paul, London).

A review of the main trends in Russian educational thinking from Peter the Great to Soviet times. Useful for setting the present system in its historical context.

Johnson, William H. E., *Russia's Educational Heritage* (1969, Octagon, New York).

This study of pre-revolutionary Russian education is especially helpful in showing how educational policy in Tsarist Russia swung from enlightenment to reaction several times, and in pointing out the connections with later developments.

King, Edmund J., ed., *Communist Education* (1963, Methuen, London).

This collection of essays deals mainly with various aspects of Soviet education, though a brief glance is also cast at Poland, East Germany, and China. The standard of the contributions is uneven, and there is considerable overlapping, but the book as a whole contains some useful material.

Select Bibliography

Kondakov, M. I., *Education in the U.S.S.R.*, (Foreign Languages Publishing House, Moscow).

A forty-eight-page outline of the educational system from the official point of view. It relies rather heavily on broad generalizations, but is useful as a summary. No date is given, but it obviously deals with the post-1958 system.

Korolev, F., *Education in the U.S.S.R.* (Soviet News Booklet No. 24, London).

This is also a brief (eighty-seven pages) description of the system from the official standpoint. Read with caution (it is unhelpfully vague on some important points such as teachers' salaries), it gives a bird's-eye view of the pre-1958 situation.

Levin, Deana, *Soviet Education Today* (1963, MacGibbon & Kee, London).

A somewhat starry-eyed view, yet useful in conveying something of the atmosphere of the Soviet schools. The author taught for five years in the U.S.S.R., and has visited extensively since then.

Noah, Harold, *Financing Soviet Schools* (1966, Teachers College, Columbia University, New York).

An excellent study of a fundamental aspect of the school system.

Noah, Harold (ed. and trans.), *The Economics of Education in the U.S.S.R.* (1969, Praeger, New York).

Twenty-four articles by Soviet authors on economics of education, based on a special conference in Moscow in 1964.

Nozhko, K., Monoszon, E., Zhamin, V., and Severtsev, V., *Educational Planning in the U.S.S.R.* (1968, UNESCO, Paris).

A study by four Soviet authors of various aspects of 'educational planning; contains some useful statistical material, apart from the analyses.

Redl, Helen B., *Soviet Educators on Soviet Education* (1964, Collier-Macmillan, London and New York).

This collection of readings from Soviet sources has some particularly useful sections on child-rearing, the family, boarding schools and extra-curricular matters.

Rosen, Seymour, *Education and Modernization in the U.S.S.R.*, (Addison-Wesley, Reading, Massachusetts, 1972).

A useful survey, particularly helpful in the interpretation (and the pitfalls) of the official statistics.

Select Bibliography

Rosen, Seymour, *Education in the U.S.S.R.: Recent Legislation and Statistics*, (U.S. Department of Health, Education and Welfare, Washington D.C., 1975).

A largely factual summary of legislation and statistics, with useful indications of where more detailed material can be obtained. Commentary ranges from the penetrating to the naïve.

Price, Ronald F., *Marx and Education in Russia and China*, (Croom Helm, London and Rowman and Littlefield, Totowa, N.J., 1977).

An excellent comparative study of the theoretical bases of Soviet and Chinese educational policy and practice, by an author with a sound and extensive knowledge of Marxism as well as experience and linguistic competence in the two countries.

Rudman, Herbert C., *The School and State in the U.S.S.R.* (1967, Macmillan, New York).

Somewhat dated with respect to the school system, this book nevertheless gives some useful information on the administration of the system, from central to local government level, and on the internal organizations of institutions and schools.

Shapovalenko, S. G. (ed.), *Polytechnical Education in the U.S.S.R.* (1963, UNESCO, Paris).

A detailed account prepared for UNESCO by the Academy of Pedagogical Sciences of the R.S.F.S.R., written as an official exposition for a foreign audience.

Tomiak, J. J., *The Soviet Union*, (David and Charles, World Education Series, London 1972).

A short but clear and useful summary; particularly helpful on the historical background.

U.S. Office of Education, *Education in the U.S.S.R.* (U.S. Office of Education Bulletin 1957, No. 14).

A mainly factual account of the Soviet system before the 1958 reforms. Comments and comparisons are kept to a minimum.

Yelyutin, V. P., *Higher Education in the U.S.S.R.* (1959, Soviet Booklet No. 51, London).

A brief survey, aimed at the foreign reader, by the Minister of Higher Education of the U.S.S.R.

Glossary of Russian Terms

Akademik: Academician. Member of the Academy of Pedagogic Sciences of the R.S.F.S.R. (q.v.), the Academy of Sciences of the U.S.S.R., etc.

Akademiya pedagogicheskikh nauk RSFSR: Academy of Pedagogic Sciences of the R.S.F.S.R. The most influential body for educational research and popularization. Recently re-organized as the Academy of Pedagogic Sciences of the U.S.S.R.

Aspirant: A post-graduate student in higher education, studying for the *Kandidat* degree (q.v.).

Assistent: Assistant lecturer (in an institution of higher education).

Attestat zrelosti: Certificate of Maturity, awarded to students successfully completing a general secondary course. It entitles them to apply for admission to higher education, but is not in itself enough.

Chlen-korrespondent: Corresponding member of an Academy (q.v.).

Chornaya rabota: Black work, i.e. manual labour.

Deistvitel'nye chleny: Full members of an Academy (q.v.).

Dekan: Dean. Head of a faculty in an institution of higher education.

Desyatiletnyaya shkola: Ten-year school. A combination of eight-year and secondary polytechnical school, giving general and polytechnical education from the age of seven to seventeen.

Detski sad: Kindergarten. The second stage of pre-school education (*doshkolnoe obrazovanie*), for children between the ages of three and seven.

Diplom: Diploma. The primary qualification awarded in higher education, the equivalent of a first degree.

Doktor nauk: Doctor of Sciences. The highest academic degree.

Dotsent: Reader or senior lecturer in an institution of higher education.

Druzhina: Brigade, e.g., of Pioneers. The School Pioneer unit.

Glossary of Russian Terms

Fakul'tet: Faculty. The primary subdivision of an institution of higher education. Each faculty deals with one subject or group of related subjects, e.g. Geology, History, Languages.

Feldsher: A second-grade medical practitioner, somewhere between a nurse and a qualified doctor.

Guligan: Hooligan. A rather wide term used to describe juvenile and other delinquents who resort to rowdyism or violence.

Institut: Institute. A higher educational establishment dealing with one speciality or group of specialities, e.g. teacher training, economics, law, technology.

Kafedra: Chair. A department within a faculty (q.v.).

Kandidat nauk: Candidate of Sciences. The first post-graduate degree, roughly equivalent to a Ph.D.

Kandidat pedagogicheskikh nauk: Candidate of pedagogic sciences. The first post-graduate degree for teachers.

Kharakteristika: Character reference, required of applicants to institutions of higher education.

Komsomol: Also known as the *V L K S M*. The senior branch of the youth movement, for young people between fifteen and twenty-seven years.

Komsomolskaya Pravda: Komsomol Truth. The national newspaper of the Komsomol organization.

Molodaya Gvardiya: Young Guard. The Komsomol publishing house.

Molodoy Kommunist: Young Communist. The Komsomol monthly journal.

Nachal'naya shkola: Elementary school, for children between the ages of seven and eleven. The elementary school is now usually organized in the same building as an incomplete secondary school, the whole being known as an eight-year school (*Vosmiletnyaya shkola*, q.v.).

Nachalnoe obrazovanie: Elementary education (*v. supra*).

Nepolnoe srednee obrazovanie: Incomplete secondary education. The stage of schooling from eleven to fifteen, usually in the fifth to eighth forms of the eight-year school (q.v.).

Obshchestvovedenie: Social studies. A course in current affairs and Marxist–Leninist theory given to senior pupils in Soviet schools.

Otryad: Detachment. A unit of the Pioneer Organization, based on the school class.

Pedagogicheskie chteniya: Pedagogic readings, contests organized by the Academy of Pedagogic Sciences, where educational papers are read in public, and the best ones published.

Pedagogicheskie instituty: Pedagogic institutes. Teacher training colleges, which train specialists for secondary schools and, to an increasing degree, for elementary schools as well.

Pedagogicheskie uchilishcha: Pedagogic schools. Specialized secondary schools (q.v.) which train teachers for elementary schools and kindergartens. Students from eight-year schools study for three or four years, those who have completed secondary education for two or three. Functions of this kind of establishment will eventually be taken over by the pedagogic institutes (*v. supra*).

Personal'nye immennye stipendii: Personal stipends. Commemorative scholarships which make extra money available to outstanding students in higher education.

Pervoe sentyabrya: First of September. On this date the schools open for the new session.

Pioner: Pioneer. The monthly magazine of the Pioneer Organization.

Pionerskaya Pravda: Pioneer Truth. The National Pioneer newspaper.

Politekhnicheskoe obrazovanie: Polytechnical education. Education based on the fundamentals of industrial and agricultural production. Not to be confused with trade training, which is vocationally biased.

Polnoe srednee obrazovanie: Complete secondary education, leading to the Certificate of Maturity (*Attestat zrelosti*, q.v.).

Prepodavatel': Lecturer in an institution of higher education.

Professional'no-tekhnicheskoe uchilishche: Vocational technical school or trade school. It provides training in a particular trade skill for young workers who have completed eight-year schooling. The course varies from six months to three years.

Profsoyuz rabotnikov prosveshicheniya, vysshei shkoly i nauchnykh uchrezhdenii S S S R: Trade Union of workers in education, higher schools, and scientific research of the U.S.S.R. The educational trade union, embracing all types and levels from an Academician to a school canteen cook.

Semestr: Term. Half of an academic year.

Semya i shkola: Family and School. A monthly magazine for parents, published by the Academy of Pedagogic Sciences of the R.S.F.S.R. (q.v.).

Shkola internat: Boarding school.

Shkola prodlennogo dnya: Prolonged day school. A modified version of the boarding school. The children stay at school during the afternoons and for meals, but go home in the evenings.

Sotrudnik: Research worker (in higher education).

Sovietskaya pedagogika: Soviet Pedagogy. The monthly journal of the Academy of Pedagogic Sciences (q.v.).

Srednie spetsial'nye uchebnye zavedeniya: Secondary specialized educational establishments. Middle schools which provide general education and training for various semi-professional occupations. Students from eight-year schools study for four years, those with complete secondary schooling for two.

Srednyaya politekhnicheskaya shkola: Secondary polytechnical school, a complete secondary school giving polytechnical and general education leading to the Certificate of Maturity. The full title is 'secondary general educational labour polytechnical school' (*srednyaya obshcheobrazovatel'naya trudovaya politekhnicheskaya shkola*).

Srednyaya shkola: Secondary school. The stage of schooling from the fifth form (age eleven) onwards.

Stazhnik: Student who has worked for at least two years between school and entering higher education.

Stilyaga: Style-follower, 'zoot-suiter', spiv – there is no exact equivalent. The term is applied to youths who are exclusively concerned with smart dressing and extreme fashion. They are regarded as social parasites and often spoken of along with juvenile delinquents.

Svobodnyi diplom: Free diploma. A diploma from an institution of higher education awarded to certain categories of graduates. It exempts the holder from the obligation to work where sent by the authorities for two or three years.

Tekhnikum: A name used for some secondary specialized schools (q.v.).

Trudovoe obuchenie: Labour training.

Uchitel'skaya gazeta: The Teachers' Newspaper. A thrice-weekly newspaper for teachers published jointly by the U.S.S.R. Ministry of Education and the Educational Trade Union.

Uchonyi soviet: Academic council. The governing body of an institution of higher education. It exists also at faculty level.

VAK (*Vysshaya attestatsionnaya kommissiya*): Higher Qualification Commission. This body confirms the award of higher degrees on behalf of the Ministry of Higher and Secondary Specialized Education. It was set up in 1938.

Vestnik vysshei shkoly: Higher School Herald. The monthly journal of the U.S.S.R. Ministry of Higher and Secondary Specialized Education.

VLKSM (*Vsesoyuznyi Leninskii Kommunisticheskii Soyuz Molodyozhi*): All-Union Leninist Communist League of Youth. Full title of the Komsomol (q.v.).

Vos'miletnyaya shkola: Eight-year school. The basic unit in the Soviet school system, it provides elementary and incomplete secondary education from seven to fifteen. Its full designation is 'Incomplete secondary general educational labour polytechnical school' (*Nepolnaya srednyaya obshcheobrazovatel'naya trudovaya politekhnicheskaya shkola*).

Voprosy psikhologii: Problems of Psychology. A specialist journal published by the Academy of Pedagogic Sciences.

Vospitatel': Upbringer. An auxiliary member of staff in a boarding school, nursery, kindergarten, etc.

Vsegda gotov: Always ready (The Pioneer motto).

Vsesoyuznaya Pionerskaya Organizatsiya imeni V. I. Lenina: All-Union Pioneer Organization named after V. I. Lenin. The branch of the Soviet youth movement for children between the ages of ten and fifteen.

VUZ (*Vyshee Uchebnoe Zavedenie*): Institution of Higher Education.

Vysshee obrazovanie: Higher education.

Yasli: Nursery, crèche. The first stage of pre-school education, for children up to the age of about three years.

Zaveduyushchii kafedroi: Head of a department (*kafedra*) within a faculty in an institution of higher education. Not necessarily a professor.

Zveno: Link. An informal Pioneer grouping within a detachment (*otryad*) (q.v.).

Index

Index

Index